I BELIEVE...

Living The

APOSTLES

CREED

Lester De Koster

Art work and cover design by Mark E. DeKoster

(C) Copyright 1996
Lester De Koster
ISBN 0-934874-13-1
Library of Congress Catalog Card Number: 95 - 83975

Published by Christian's Library Press, Inc.
P.O. Box 2226
Grand Rapids, MI 49501-2226

FOREWORD

It is with a high measure of enthusiasm that I contribute this brief introduction to a splendid new work on the Apostles Creed. Many books--hundreds, perhaps thousands of them--have been written over the centuries on this central confession of the Christian faith. Some are distinctly ordinary. Others are very good indeed. This volume by Lester De Koster is different from any I have ever seen. It is in a class by itself. It is <u>sui generis</u>.

I Believe...Living The Apostles Creed is a book written by a brilliant rhetorician who is also a keen student both of the Bible and of Christian thought and who, very much in the pattern of the great Augustine, places his quite wonderful gifts at the service of the church. He dedicates his work to his grandchildren. Happy are those grandchildren--and others--who may sit at his feet and receive his instruction as he reflects on the old creed as a whole and then draws out of each article the meaning intended by ancient confessors and its implications for believers today.

Dr. De Koster is not a professional theologian. He is an amateur in that discipline. When I describe him as an "amateur theologian," however, I am very far from suggesting any disrespect. Here I use the word "amateur" in its fine original sense. I apply it to him as one who studies, reflects, and writes on biblical and theological themes for the love of his discipline. That he has written this learned, comprehensive, penetrating, profound, and eminently readable book with love for God, for his subject matter, and for those whom he addresses is apparent on every page.

The thoughtful reader who embarks upon the adventure this book offers will very quickly discover why I am so very hearty in my appreciation of it. Lester De Koster --Christian scholar, disciple of John Calvin, bookman, librarian, teacher, editor, writer, divine--has brought together a lifetime of learning and experience in this jewel of a book. Its chapters are short: suitable for personal or family worship. They are also rich and full. Each stands by itself, but the progression is unmistakable, and each builds upon what has gone before.

Extraordinarily significant is the way in which the materials of the creed are tackled. Dr. De Koster begins with a highly individual and carefully developed discussion of good works in relation to faith in Jesus Christ. That part of his teaching alone will immediately capture the reader's attention. Moreover, he takes up the twelfth article in the creed first, for a very good reason!

This book is bound to do much good. It clearly has enduring value as a treatise on Christian faith and life. More than that, it is a beautiful, powerful legacy to grandchildren and others, from a man who loves and serves the Lord God with passion and is determined to do what he can to transmit the grandeur, divine simplicity, and saving grace of the gospel to the generations still to come.

Dr. John Richard de Witt
Pastor, Seventh Reformed Church
Grand Rapids, Michigan

For Ruth/Leslie

Who Urged

To Christopher, Sara, Paige, Amy, Kate, Alicia, Jonathan

"The winds of error blow freely
through the mind
unstructured by sound doctrine."

John Calvin

The Lord's Mandate To His Church:

"Go therefore and make disciples of all nations..."

(by)

"Teaching them all that I have commanded you."

Matthew 28:19-21

Table of Contents

THE APOSTLES CREED

I believe:

1.   In God the Father Almighty,
        Maker of heaven and earth.

2.   And in Jesus Christ his only begotten Son,
        our Lord;

3.   Who was conceived by the Holy Spirit,
        born of the Virgin Mary;

4.   Suffered under Pontius Pilate; was crucified,
        dead, and buried;

5.   He descended into hell; the third day
        he rose from the dead;

6.   He ascended into heaven, and sits on the right
        hand of God the Father Almighty;

7.   From thence he shall come to judge
        the living and the dead.

I believe:

8.   In the Holy Spirit.

9.   A holy catholic Church,
        the communion of saints;

10. The forgiveness of sins;

11. The resurrection of the body;

12. And the life everlasting.

                              Amen.

Companions of angels, friends of stars, living Image-bearers of the living God! Of infinite possibility.

Who, me?

Yes, you!

You have no idea of your true value. None of us has. Nor of how unique a self each of you is. None of us fully understands. You are you, and there is no duplicate. None! Never! What you are making of you is the only edition there is ever going to be. And the product you are turning out, the self you are sculpting in every choice you make, lasts forever.

There are so many of us humans, the whole earth filling up with us at an alarming pace, that it's hard to believe that you and I and everyone else can matter much, especially to God the Creator.

But you do!

God knows each of you by name. Just as He knows the stars. And no one, but God, knows just how many stars there are: *"He determines the number of the stars, he gives all of them their names"* (Psalm 147:4). That's a parable. If He knows the stars by name because He made and sustains them, so He knows each of His Image-bearers. It's said that no two snowflakes are exactly alike. There's no counting them in a blizzard either. God knows. He designs them.

Stars and snowflakes come as teachers. Look and learn! God sustains each of them as unique--no copies. So also He designs you to be...you--no second editions. You can't make yourself unique. You are! For you life means working that out. What kind of you is it going to be? God's kind? The kind He profiles in His Word, the Bible? The kind of you destined to enjoy Him forever? Or, alas, some other kind? That's what life is given you to determine.

So, don't try to make yourself some one special. You are! You don't have to catch the fickle public eye. God's eye is the one that counts, and His eye is ever upon each of us: *"In him we live, and move, and have our being"* (Acts 17:28).

Because He wishes us to become the true persons He has made us to be, God always treats us as persons. This means that He makes us free to choose or reject His way for living. This is the meaning of the choices of all kinds that we make every day. How He makes free choice possible for us is the content of the Apostles Creed.

Come, see!

Think of it as written and kept just for you!

It is the most widely used and concise summary of the heart of Christianity. As hearts do, this Creed offers to pump the life-giving blood of divine Truth through your every artery.

Learn to see yourself mirrored in the Truth the Creed confesses. We will talk about doing that.

It has just twelve articles. Meaning that this Creed was, as its name suggests, written by Christ's twelve Apostles, maybe?

No one seems to know for sure. There are some who even assign the various articles to various Apostles, substituting Matthias for Judas, of course (as reported in the Acts, 1:26). There are many more who believe that the name Apostles Creed implies the teaching of the Apostles rather than their authorship. No matter, really, so far as we are concerned.

The Creed lays the foundation, or rather reports the foundation laid by God for His treating you as persons. Meaning that God treats all of us as free to choose for, or against, Him.

The Bible puts that as a choice between "life" and "death." The Creed points us to life, now and forever.

Let's start with where you are at this moment.

To live is to act. To act involves choice. You choose to do or not do this or that or something else. "Act" includes everything--what we think, what we say, what we busy ourselves in. Even trying to do nothing is an act. We pave the way of life in acts, and so point our way to heaven or hell. And every choice to do, or not to do, shapes who we are making our-selves to be. In fact that is why God gives us days--so we can become ourselves. You might think of your choices as each one chipping away at the sculpture of your self. Only you can do it. Every choice a chip. Or, if you like, think of your every choice as adding a touch to the portrait of your self you are painting, in bright glowing colors or otherwise. You the artist; your self the work of art. With every choice as the brush.

Do we sculpt or paint the self we are becoming with choices made on our own whim? made because everybody is doing this or that?

Or by way of choices made according to the rules God lays down for those who would be His children? He makes that possible for us. The Creed tells how.

The Apostles Creed summarizes the foundation steps taken by God in establishing the world and putting Christianity in it. It profiles what God has done and is doing in Jesus Christ and through the Holy Spirit to: 1) liberate all who believe from bondage to the world, the flesh and the Devil, so that, 2) by faith they can realize in themselves the Image of God in which they are made, and in so doing serve God's purposes in history.

That is what Christianity, as profiled by the Creed, is first of all for, with consequences flowing out to revolutionize history.

And how does Christianity go about achieving that end?

After the model established by Jesus Himself. He chose and instructed disciples. They were hand-picked to occupy a special office as founders of the New Testament Church. And then in His so-called "Great Commission," Jesus sends the Church out into the world with a mandate focused on us; consider it coming to you by name. Jesus says: *"Go therefore and make disciples of all nations, baptizing them in the name of the Father and of the Son and of the Holy Spirit, teaching them to observe all that I have commanded you; and lo, I am with you always, to the close of the age"* (Mat. 28:19-20). Jesus will stand with those who obey.

Christianity is in the world to make you a disciple. The Church is in the world to facilitate that by teaching you to do all that the Lord, through His word, commands. Through baptism you received the triune God as sponsor of your discipleship. God the Father acts through the office of the Elder in the Church; God the Son acts through the office of the Minister in the Church; God the Holy Spirit acts through the office of the Deacon in the Church. All collaborate to one end: making you the Lord's disciple by teaching you to do all that the Lord commands, thus effecting your salvation and impacting your world.

Doing what the Lord commands consists in what the Bible calls "good works." We can will to do good works because of the liberation wrought for us in Jesus as outlined by the Creed.

Because He has made good works possible, Jesus is coming at the end of time to judge just how obedient each of us has been: *"For the Son of Man is to come with his angels in the glory of his Father, and then he will repay every man for what he has done"* (Mat. 16:27). This is Jesus' own description. Remember! Always!

The goal of the Creed is to place upon our lips a confession of faith in all that God has done to open before us a discipleship rich in social consequences, *"Thy kingdom come...."*

Thus your life gets meaning. There is no other way.

Our Confession Of:

What God Has Done - And Is Doing - So We By Faith Can

Will To Do His Will, And Thus Become Jesus' Disciples,

Here, Now, And Forever!

In ways the Bible describes, like these:

1. *"Christ, who has been raised from the dead in order that we may bear fruit for God"* (Romans 7:4).

2. *"Let your light so shine before men that they may see your good works and give glory to your Father who is in heaven"* (Matthew 5:16).

3. *"Jesus Christ gave himself for us to redeem us from all iniquity and to purify for himself a people of his own who are zealous for good works"* (Titus 2:14).

4. *"For we are his workmanship, created in Christ Jesus for good works, which God prepared before-hand, that we should walk in them"* (Ephesians 2:10).

5. *"All scripture is inspired by God and profitable for teaching, for reproof, for correction, and for training in righteousness, that everyone who belongs to God may be complete, equipped for every good work"* (IITimothy 3:16-17).

In the famous third book of his Institutes, where he writes what has been called "The Golden Booklet Of The Christian Life," John Calvin lists some of the texts we have just quoted. Then he goes on to say, "Those few Scriptural proofs, indeed, I have set forth as a mere taste. For if it were my purpose to go through every one, a large volume might be compiled. All of the apostles are full of exhortations, urgings, reproofs with which to instruct us in every good work, and that without mention of merit" (Inst. III.16.3).

We are taught by Jesus to pray for a "kingdom" on earth where we as citizens aim at doing God's will here as it is done in heaven: *"Thy kingdom come, Thy will be done, on earth as it is in heaven"* (Mat. 6:10), beginning of course with the one who prays.

And now we are in the middle of a long dispute. You notice that Calvin concludes with what might be a puzzling phrase, "and that without mention of merit." Why does he say that?

Calvin has in view this question: can good works, whatever they are, earn us life eternal? Are they the merit badges, so to speak, which taken together land us in heaven? Is that what the Creed is about?

Or is heaven attained through "faith alone," as Luther (mis-) translates Romans 5:1? Or, are faith and works even at odds, the one ruling out the other?

Famous names are in on this discussion, Luther and John Wesley and George Whitfield and lots of crusade evangelists in our own time, all for "faith alone." Calvin is not among them. For him it's no problem. It must not be for you.

God's Image is realized in us by way of good works. That of course is why He asks us to choose to do them. Let's repeat what Calvin says: "All of the apostles are full of exhortations, urgings, reproofs with which to instruct the man of God in every good work, <u>and that without mention of merit</u>."

In short, why are we called to doing good works? Answer: <u>because God commands them</u> for incarnating His Image in us and expanding His influence in our world. "Are you saved?" simply means "are you choosing to obey God's will in good works?" Not to earn heaven. No one is talking about earning heaven. Perhaps some people put the issue that way just to say, "Of course, we can't earn heaven anyway," and then dismiss God's demand for good works altogether. Don't do that! He wants us to be "zealous for good works!" The Bible repeatedly says so!

God designs good works as, so to speak, our footsteps to Himself and His footprints in history. And as we thus are permitted to experience Him, there is heaven! Good works are the Way! The self we sculpt in acts of obedience is the self destined for "life." How this is possible is what the Creed summarizes for us.

So, dear children, never waste your time in arguing whether or not good works <u>earn</u> heaven. You may be sure that such argument does not count as a good work: *"For the kingdom of heaven does not consist in talk but in power"* (I Cor. 4:20). Talk is fun, but God's power works in us through our obedient behavior. O yes, we can't make it on our own. And we will come to the crucial role of the Holy Spirit in our will to obey. But remember always Paul's warning, *"Do not be deceived; God is not mocked, for whatever we sow that shall we also reap"* (Gal. 6:7). That's why being "saved" means being "zealous for good works."

Let the Light of God's Word come to focus upon ourselves here.

1. *"Christ, who has been raised from the dead in order that we may bear fruit for God"* (Rom. 7:4). But, IF we do not will to "bear fruit for God," then was Christ raised from the dead for us?

2. *"Let your light so shine before men that they may see your good works and give glory to your Father who is in heaven"* (Mat. 5:16). Our good works glorify, not ourselves, but God. If we do no "good works" we rob God of a "glory" He clearly expects from us.

3) *"Jesus Christ gave himself for us to redeem us from all iniquity and to purify for himself a people of his own zealous for good works"* (Titus 2:34). But if we are not "zealous for good works," then did Jesus Christ give himself for us? Have we been purified "from all iniquity" if we do no "good works" to show it?

4) *"For we are his workmanship, created in Christ Jesus for good works, which God prepared beforehand that we should walk in them"* (Eph. 2:10). But, if we in fact do not will to do "good works," what evidence do we show of being God's "workmanship"?

5) *"All scripture is inspired by God and profitable for teaching, for reproof, for correction, and for training in righteousness, that everyone who belongs to God may be complete, equipped for every good work"* (II Timothy 3:16-17). Now, quite frankly, if in fact we show no "good works" what reason do we have for believing that we do "belong to God"? Did He in fact, so far as we are concerned, inspire the Scripture in vain?

St. James sums it up in his well-known aphorism, *"Faith without works is dead"* (Jas. 2:20). "To believe is to obey," writes Dietrich Bonhoeffer, German pastor martyred for opposing Hitler, "and to obey is to believe."

God speaks to us as He spoke to Israel through the lips of Moses: *"I call heaven and earth to witness against you this day, that I have set before you life and death, blessing and curse; therefore choose life, that you and your descendants may live, loving the Lord your God, obeying his voice, and cleaving to him; for that means life to you and length of days, that you may dwell in the land which the Lord sware to your fathers, to Abraham, to Isaac, and to Jacob, to give them"* (Deut. 30:19-20).

Therefore, children, choose life in loving God, which is obedience to His Word, which is doing good works. And He will give us the "promised land," the symbol for life eternal with Him in heaven. Pray often, because you mean it, "Thy kingdom come, Thy will be done, on earth..." through me! Draw power for it from the Creed.

What are "good works"?

A moment or two to say, a lifetime to do.

We can learn something about good works from an ancient and simple distinction. It's between "potency" and "act." Aristotle dealt with that four centuries before Christ; so did St. Thomas Aquinas twelve centuries after Him. So do philosophers today. Looks obscure. But helpful. What you can do is potency; what you do is act, be it mental or physical.

Imagine yourself fast asleep. You are not dreaming, so far as you know. Nothing seems to be going on. "You" are off somewhere. But imagine all the things you might be doing, if you were awake, like thinking, imagining, feeling, speaking, getting up and doing this or that, running or jumping--endless possibilities. You couldn't even catalog all the "acts" you are potentially capable of doing. Let's call that your potency, your ability to act.

Then suppose you do awake. Acts begin. Thoughts begin to flow. Imagination looks to this or that. You begin to phrase thoughts in words and speak them to yourself or to someone. You choose to do something. Potency becomes action.

What's the difference between you asleep, and you awake? We can say that it's the difference between potency and act, between what you can do and what you do. Think of potency as taking on incarnation in act. Whether it's what you think, what you say, or what you do, to live is to clothe potency with act-uality. We may call it doing a "work."

Every act, mental or physical, is in biblical terms a "work."

And "works" come in only two varieties, good or bad. What's the difference? The good are done in harmony with God's revealed will; the bad are done in rebellion against it. The Lord's true disciple, what you are called to be, seeks to learn God's will and tries to obey it. That's what the Bible and its teaching in the Church are for.

Christianity is the religion of incarnation, the incarnation of the Son, the Word of God, in Jesus Christ; and in a parallel way, the incarnation of God's biblical Word through our acts in "works." That is what Jesus came to make possible. That is what the Creed is about.

In a nutshell: to live is potency; to act is giving your potential incarnation in works; good works are those acts which are obedient to the will of God as revealed through His Word. We need not speak of the others. Don't!!

You see that it's never a matter of doing, or not doing, "works."

Whatever we do is a "work." Doing in whatever form, be it mental or physical, is bringing potency out of possibility into reality. You can look back on the day, every day, as filled with "works."

You will see that it does not make much sense to ask yourself if you want to do works. Doing works is what living is. What matters is not if we do works, but what kind they are. Jesus calls them fruit: *"Either make the tree good, and its fruit good; or make the tree bad, and its fruit bad; for the tree is known by its fruit.... Do men gather grapes of thorns, or figs of thistles? Even so every good tree brings forth good fruit; but a corrupt tree brings forth evil fruit. A good tree cannot bring forth evil fruit, neither can a corrupt tree bring forth good fruit. Every tree that brings not forth good fruit is hewn down, and cast into the fire. Wherefore by their fruits you shall know them"* (Mat. 7:15-20).

Who we are is revealed by our works. Our acts tell whose servant we are, God's or Satan's. There are no other options.

Our "good works" are the fruit in our daily living produced by God's Word taking possession of us and becoming incarnate in our acts. God's Word does that through our "I believe...."

Don't suppose that you are expected to sit down, as Benjamin Franklin says in his Autobiography that he did, to make your own list of good works and then to pursue doing them. Go to the Bible. The inspired Word is full of the "You shall..." and "You shall not...!" Moreover, the Bible not only defines good works, it does far more. The Bible empowers us to do them through the Spirit. Our "I believe" is a commitment to let the Word take possession of us. We go, therefore, to the Bible to learn what "good works" are, and to find the Power to pursue them. That is what Paul means by saying that *"All scripture is inspired by God"* to the end that we, who believe what we hear there can be *"equipped for every good work"* (II Tim. 3:16-17). The Bible defines and, through the Spirit, empowers obedience.

In sum: to live is to act. To act in the form of good works is the fruit of opening ourselves to control by God's inspired Word. Turn always to the Bible to learn and to do what God asks of those in whom He chooses to restore His Image.

And if we want to know what kind of "tree" we are, as life goes along, Jesus provides us with a remarkable mirror for judging our progress. It's called the Sermon on the Mount, Matthew chapters 5 through 7. As you read it, ask: "Am I like that?" Be ever hopeful that some of that is rubbing off. And keep at it!

First Step

We can now see why Jesus sets our first step into discipleship at self-denial. It's His Word, not our ideas that must shape our lives. We must more and more get self, and self-interest, and selfishness, out of the way! That's hard work. Doesn't come over-night. But Jesus is firm about it: *"Then Jesus told his disciples, 'If any one would come after me, let him deny himself and take up his cross and follow me'"* (Mat. 16:24). There is no exception: *"...and he who does not take his cross and follow me is not worthy of me"* (Mat. 10:38). "Take up your cross," He says. The cross is the instrument of death. The gate of self-denial, the road of getting self-interest out of the way runs counter to our natural inclinations. Not everyone manages it. That is what He means by saying that *"the gate is narrow and the way is hard that leads to life, and those who find it are few"* (Mat. 7:14). Can you?

Some forms of evangelism offer heaven by appealing to our self-interest in salvation. Being "saved" is like reaching out your open palm for freebies. No narrow gate and no hard way. Only "accepting Christ" by side-stepping His demand for self-denying obedience. That is not the Lord's prescribed Way! We shall observe that frequently as the Creed moves us along.

A sound evangelism calls us to discipleship, saying in effect: "You accept the cross of self-denial and pray that Christ will 'accept' your will to do His will by giving you His Spirit."

It is possible to read the Creed, to repeat the Creed, to memorize the Creed without ever intending to let it take control. Without ever acknowledging it as prepared by divine Providence across the ages to bear fruit in your lives by way of taking posses-sion of you and all your are. But that is the only way to "profit" from its boundless riches. Here in twelve succinct articles is the beating heart of Christianity. It profiles what was summed up by our Lord Himself: *"For God so loved the world that he gave his only Son, that whoever believes in him should not perish but have eternal life"* (John 3:16). The Creed details this divine "giving."

Our Lord warns against missing the point: *"And this is the judgment, that the light has come into the world, and people loved darkness rather than light, because their deeds were evil. For everyone who does evil hates the light, and does not come to the light, lest his deeds be exposed"* (John 3:19-20).

We are going to see that Jesus always confronts us with an "either/or"--obedience and life, or disobedience and death. Either a life dedicated to good works or one wasted away into destruction.

It's the challenge given through Moses long ago, *"Therefore, choose life!"* (Deut. 30:19). How God makes that choice possible is detailed by the Creed. We will start at the top!

Article 12.

AND THE LIFE EVERLASTING.

We will begin with this

grand climax of the Creed,

letting it beckon us as a beacon

along the Way.

With Article 12 the Creed has reached its goal. It has taken us by the hand and led us through time to the gates of eternity, where angels sing and Jesus awaits: *"For now we see through a glass darkly, but then face to face"* (I Cor. 15:12). Lovers of poetry might look at Book III of Dante's great <u>Divine Comedy</u>, where he imagines what heaven will be like. It's called <u>The Paradiso</u>.

You sense at once that if it takes eleven articles of the Creed to bring us at last to eternal life, then our salvation is a Way of many steps. The Bible offers no short-cuts to heaven. Instead it measures our every choice along the path of life for its contribution to that "book" of our lives which will be opened on the Last Day for judgment (Rev. 20:12-13).

For those whose "I believe..." is sincere, whose will to self-denial is genuine, whose faith opens to the Word, there awaits God's own, *"Well done, good and faithful servant, you have been faithful over a little, I will set you over much; enter into the joy of your master"* (Mat. 25:21): the life everlasting!

The possibility of hearing that for yourself envelops life with meaning. It's what living is for; what <u>Christianity</u> is for; what the Bible and the Creed are all about. It's what our day by day living must finally add up to: *"Strive to enter in...by the strait gate and the narrow way,"* our Lord commands (Mat. 7:13-14).

Jesus Himself directs our sober attention to the theme of Article 12. He says: *"Labor not for the food that perishes, but for the food which endures to eternal life, which the Son of Man will give you"* (John 6:27). Think about that. He says it to you!

St. Paul echoes Him: *"For he [God] will render to every one according to his works: to those who by patience in well-doing seek for glory and honor and immortality, he will give eternal life"* (Rom. 2:6-7). Are you listening? and hearing?

Consider two things carefully:

1) *"Eternal life,"* the *"life everlasting,"* is gift. Jesus: *"which the Son of Man will give you."* Paul: *"he [God] will give (you)."* We cannot earn life eternal. We don't need to. God gives it. But, to whom does He give it?

2) Listen carefully: God <u>gives</u> eternal life with one staggering, but challenging, IF! It's an IF which covers the whole of our lives and gives meaning to our every act. God gives us life everlasting, IF, according to Jesus, we "labor" for it; or IF, as explained by Paul, we are "patient in well-doing." Nothing said about coming forward, raising the hand, "accepting" the Savior. Nothing at all! No "four laws" and easy steps either. No gimmicks.

17

Does it seem puzzling?

IF eternal life is God's gift, WHY do Jesus and Paul insist that we must "labor" in "well-doing" for it? Must you earn a gift?

Consider carefully: earn it, no. A gift is a gift. But what if we have to qualify for it, say? That is how Jesus and Paul put it.

We are dealing here with a biblical paradox. There are others. We will talk about biblical paradox later. Here we are told, unmistakably, to work for what God will give. The logic, on our terms, may be puzzling, self-contradictory maybe. But Jesus tells us what is going on by way of a familiar parable:

"For it will be as when a man going on a journey called his servants and entrusted to them his property; to one he gave five talents, to another two, and to another one, to each according to his ability." Talents measure money, like our dollars and cents (Mat. 25:14-30).

While the master is away, the servant who received five talents, and the one who received two talents, busied themselves with developing their capital. They put the talents into good work. As result, each doubled the master's gift.

So, when the master returns and takes account of his servants' success, he rewards them: *"Well done, good and faithful servant, you have been faithful over a little, I will set you over much; enter into the joy of your master."* They had qualified themselves for the master's ultimate gift.

Those servants are like ourselves. What they had to work with was not their own creation; it was God's gift. So with His gifts to us of life, time and abilities; all are divine investment in us.

We may judge that the servants did work prescribed by their Master, good work. So must we.

Now observe the result. The servants who multiplied their gift of talents thus qualified themselves for the ultimate gift. They did not earn the final reward. They simply used the talents to show themselves qualified to receive the larger gift: *"You have been faithful over a little; I will set you over much."*

Such is the function of our obedient good works. They do not earn eternal life. God graciously counts them as showing us qualified to receive His gift of it.

Earn? No! But qualify? By all means. Remember the difference.

Before we consider the judgment upon the unprofitable servant, let's reflect on the crucial significance of this parable for us.

We are going to consider, a little later, what may be called the sacramental character of our universe. That is what the creation became after man's disobedience and Fall in the Garden of Eden. We will come to a closer look at that awful event.

A sacrament is a secular thing given a sacred meaning. Sometimes the Church's sacraments, like baptism and the Holy Supper, are called earthly things with heavenly meaning.

That is precisely what the creation became when Adam and Eve were expelled from the Garden of Eden. The account is in Genesis, chapters 2 and 3. We will summarize it as an "Interim," below. That is, after man's Fall, God decided that how we use His world, and our talents, and how we treat ourselves and others, would be sacramental--temporal acts with eternal meaning. The self we are creating out of all our temporal choices in the world is destined for eternity. Our destiny is determined by our use of God's gifts of life, time, talent and world. We make the world sacramental. That is, no act of ours is without eternal consequence. So God made the world after our first parents fell from communion with Him.

This explains the parable. Each servant, just like each of us, is entrusted with life, time, and talent to make sacramental his every act. Those who do devote themselves to service of the Master qualify for reward. They have sacramentalized God's gifts.

God gives us opportunity to use time, talents and circumstances to qualify ourselves for His gift of everlasting life. The alternative is refusal to obey. That is the form taken by eternal death.

The servant who had received the one talent was a surly chap. He declined to sacramentalize his master's gift, and buried it in the ground. Jesus is surely teaching us that refusal to do good works is like that. We in effect bury God's gifts by refusing to use them in obedience to His will.

This totally selfish and unproductive servant goes to hell. Why? Because he does no good works! The master calls him *"a wicked and slothful servant,"* strips him of his talent and condemns him to be *"cast into the outer darkness, where there will be weeping and gnashing of teeth"* (Mat. 25:30).

Notice how vividly here Jesus sets before us the alternatives: obey and receive reward in life eternal; or disobey into eternal damnation. No half-way house between! Sacramentalize your life and world, or lose them.

Let us modestly try to parallel the parable of the talents. Just suppose that some stranger dropped by your house one day with a present. He comes to offer you one of the world's great violins, say one made by the Italian master Stradivarius. What will you do?

"I have come to give it to you," the stranger says.

"But I can't play," you respond. "How shall I ever qualify myself even to accept, let alone deserve, such a gift?"

The stranger has a ready answer. You can, he says, develop your talents for the violin. He even has a book of instructions for training what he says are your inborn talents for learning to play. Still more, he has an institute for training you by evoking and maturing those innate capacities. He even hints at some mysterious Power who, he says, will actually work within you to learn and practice the skills you need. All you need do is sign on, and try.

"And after you go through the course," he says, "I will give you the instrument as yours forever. All I ask of you is the will to qualify for this gift. All you need offer is the desire to follow my program. I do the rest."

Well, you do get the point, of course, of this humble parable.

The stranger is God. He offers you the gift of life eternal, if you will really try to qualify yourself to receive it. That's represented by the violin.

His Training Manual is obviously the Bible. His training institute is the Church. Calvin frequently speaks of the Bible as God's "school," with the Church as the teacher. Or of the Bible as the Lord's scepter, the Word through which He governs the acts of would-be disciples. Jesus assigns the Church, in the person of His disciples, the task of *"teaching them [believers] to do all I have commanded you"* (Mat. 28:20). And you must of course study on your own too. Such training is in principle quite simple. The Bible is inspired to put God's Word in control of your self. We do not master God's Word; we experience salvation as His Word masters us. Don't let the "scholar" mislead you about that. We don't master the Bible. Either God's Word takes possession of us, or we don't know it at all. That's why we must deny our selves: to understand the Word by standing-under it.

And God offers the illumination of His Spirit. There is much to be said about that. And we will come to it. For purposes of this imaginary parable, let's just say that the Holy Spirit is God's CEO, as they say nowadays in industry, Chief Executive Officer, the living, loving link between us and God's will for our lives. We can qualify for the gift--of the violin, yes, and of eternal life!

In Article 12, the Creed declares that our end is our beginning. Death is not conclusion but prologue. Life goes on...forever!

It's the goal toward which the moments are tending for us all. Mourn their passing as we may, regret time's fleeting as we will, every passing moment is but stepping stone to this crowning glory enunciated by the Creed, "I believe the life everlasting."

St. Paul foretells it: *"When the perishable puts on the imperishable, and this mortal nature puts on immortality, then shall come to pass the saying that is written, 'Death is swallowed up in victory'"* (I Cor. 15:54, quoting Is. 25:8).

It is for this article of the Creed that Jesus says He came and took our flesh: *"I am come that you might have life, and have it more abundantly"* (John 10:10). That is, we can have life in Him now, as foretaste of life abundant with Him forever. It is now, even in the fleeting "now," that we bespeak the Creed. And it is in so doing that we already begin to experience the "life" of which Jesus speaks. We learn that the Creed maps out, so to speak, Jesus' route for getting from the "now" to the "forever."

How urgent this is becomes clear when we take note of what John the Baptist said in introducing Jesus to Israel, and the world. Speaking of why Jesus came in our flesh, John says of Him, *"Whose fan is in his hand, and he will thoroughly purge his floor, and gather his wheat into the garner; but he will burn up the chaff with unquenchable fire"* (Mat. 3:12).

Again, the either/or. The Way of obedience in willing to do the will of God leads to our in-gathering by the Lord for life in His "garner;" the way of selfish disobedience leaves us at the end as "chaff" destined for fire unquenchable. We have, obviously, no more urgent business than making sure, choice by choice, that we are walking that hard road of self-denying good works.

Jesus makes that choice possible as detailed by the Creed. Call upon Him often to guide you by Word and Spirit in setting your steps along His Way. It's not stuffy, and is "hard" only because your natural wishes so often lead you astray from it. The company of Father, Son and Holy Spirit whom you keep through knowing better and better His Word is the truest, kindest, warmest friendship you can acquire. It is, indeed, LIFE now and forever!

Here the Creed concludes with "Amen."

So let it be!!

We will go on, now, to trace the steps which bring us, at last, to life everlasting.

Article 1.

I BELIEVE IN GOD,

THE FATHER ALMIGHTY,

MAKER OF HEAVEN AND EARTH

The Creed knows us well enough.

We start with our favorite term. It's "I."

The "I" comes from the Latin term ego, meaning "I."

We talk about people with a "big ego," meaning a pretty high estimate of themselves. Such people are egoists. Those egoists who constantly talk about themselves are also egotists. They can be boring.

First thing to note about the Creed is that it serves to mirror us to ourselves. So it starts with "I." That's far more significant than you may at first suppose.

There is an ancient bit of Jewish wisdom which advises us to carry in some pocket of our memory two bits of information. One bit says,"You are the merest worm, strutting about in a world not your own as if you owned the place. Cool it!"

The other bit says, "It is for you that the world was made, that the sun treads the sky, while the universe awaits your exploration just over the horizon called death. Walk very tall!"

Both are true, and therefore useful. Each has its occasion.

There are some days that put you in need of the first, and some days that put you in need of the other. So, in the pockets of your memory you carry both, leaning on one or the other as needed to get you through what is happening right now, every day. Probably there are many days when you need both.

How those little bits can be understood rightly is taught us by the Creed. It stresses our inherent depravity, and our potential nobility.

But let's begin with our potential.

Don't suppose that whatever you know about how babies are born into the world is all there is to know about who you are. Getting born is just the observable, miracle that it is. What is most real about us is not seen on the surface of things.

We are born into the Image of God. It was so from the beginning: ***"So God created man in his own image, in the image of God created he him; male and female he created them"*** (Gen. 1:27). You, too!

Life is God-ordained opportunity to enter upon the promise of this Image, to become who we are! The Bible describes it; the Creed points the way. Follow it!

Take note that you as human beings are the only ones, except for God and the angels (so far as we know) who can say "I."

The "I" is indeed an over-worked word. So much so that the dictionary has a whole company of terms rooted in its Latin root ego. The egoist thinks always of him- or herself. The egotist talks that way. And so on. There's even egomania meaning exclusively egocentric, which means self-centered--which is depravity in full bloom. A rather common bit of flora.

But the abuse of "I" only accents its absolute centrality.

We use "I" so much because the self is, each "I" is, the hub around which our world revolves. Our senses reach out like the spokes of a wheel. Wherever and whatever they touch becomes the circumference of our experience.

The "I" is it! For each one of us! All initiative starts here. All consequences finally come home to roost here. Stage-front-and-center: the "I."

It takes the Ten Commandments to alert us to the sad doom of egomania, and the Holy Spirit to help us obey our Lord's command to "deny" our egoism and follow Him. He will, if we deny our selves, fashion of each self a new hub for our universe. That's called redemption. It's the road to acquiring a new self.

But don't let a depraved inheritance and the horrifying excesses of egomania all around us blind you to the marvelous majesty of who and what the "I"-saying creation (that's you!) really is and can be.

Marvelous examples of an "I" quietly in the service of God and society flourish about us if we have an eye for them. The soft touch, the kind word, the winsome smile, the boost in need, the sharing of smile or tear, the cheerful doing of duty or kindness--all these fruits of the Spirit of God maturing some "I" into the Image we bear are here and now. They knit the fabric of society so violently rent by other forms of the "I" intent upon denial of the Image. It's the violent who make the news, and the gentle who are hardly noticed. No matter. It's always the "I" that matters, God sorting them out into His and not-His.

It's His "I" who confesses the Creed.

Say it now: "I" BELIEVE....

Being an "I" means, as we have been saying, enjoying the Image of the "I-"saying God.

You recall that the Book of Exodus tells how God sends Moses to Egypt to lead Israel out of bondage. He speaks, you remember, out of the burning bush (that's in Exodus chapter 3).

Moses is not at all happy with that assignment. Why should he be? He had been banished from Egypt and was no doubt under abiding sentence of death there. And the Pharaoh knew very well who Moses was, after raising him as if his own grandson in the royal family.

So Moses is reluctant. He has an idea for getting off the hook. What if the people of Israel doubt his word, and ask the name of the God who sent him: *"What shall I say to them?"* And God said to Moses, *"I AM WHO I AM. And say to the people of Israel, 'I AM has sent me to you'"* (Ex. 3:13-14). That's the term expressed by the Latin ego sum: I am. It's the term you and I imply every time we say "I." So Moses went, and God liberated Israel through him.

God can say I AM, and He equips His Image-bearer to say the same. Angels can say "I" also. At least the angel Gabriel says it in frustration with the old priest Zechariah who cannot quite believe Gabriel's message that he and his aged wife Elizabeth are going to have a son--who became John the Baptist, forerunner of Jesus: *"I am Gabriel, who stand in the presence of God; and I am sent to speak to you..."* (Luke 1:19). But, angels aside, we humans are the only creatures who can say "I" and can have some awareness of what that miracle means.

Saying "I" advertises: Image-bearer of God! And each time you say it, listen for God's echo, "Now act like it!"

One of the striking things about our-selves revealed by the Bible is this: you are custodian, care-taker, of your soul. Your "soul" is you, your "I," looked at from God's perspective. You are responsible for your soul/self. You are becoming what you are making your self to be. You-I-self, all the same person.

Jesus implies it: *"For what profit is it, if one gain the whole world, and lose one's own soul?"* (Mark 8:36).

Jesus is saying that in looking at yourself you see, as it were, double. The "I" can stand off and look at the "self." It's common enough. We do it all the time. We like what we have just done or said or thought...or we don't. We sit in judgment upon our-selves. It's a form of self-consciousness. And Jesus is saying that you are in fact responsible for your-self. Your "soul" is like having an often-times rambunctious little dog on a leash: now, you just behave!

Probably only humans are capable of self-consciousness. We can set our-selves apart from our-selves, the one viewing the other. We do that when we talk to our-selves, when we "see" our-selves in situations we anticipate or which are now past. It may be the source of the feeling of shame; we "see" our-selves acting in ways we wish had not occurred, ways that embarrass us, offensive to others and to God.

Yes, the "I" is responsible for the "I." That is the meaning of freedom. It is at the heart of Christianity. Jesus Christ sacrifices Himself for those who believe so that they can accept responsibility for their own "I" in all behavior.

Shakespeare and other writers do speak of that "most precious jewel," the soul, entrusted to our care. In short, Jesus reminds us that "I" am responsible for me in a way no one else can be. Which means that the "I" is responsible for what the "I" does. Can't put the blame on anyone, or anything. Happily God will empower our exercising such awesome responsibilities, if we first assume them.

Did you notice the comparison which Jesus makes? He contrasts gaining "the whole world" with the worth of YOUR SELF!

Never thought about it that way, maybe? "I" worth more than the whole world? "I", "me," "myself" of more importance to God than all His creation? Just so! When you see a child, any child, the great Swiss educator Johann Pestalozzi said, "Fall on your knees!"

When you look in the mirror, think about it: Jesus counts you of greater importance, of greater value, as meaning more to Him, than the whole world! Can you live up to that? The Creed says you can!

Each of us is born with three servants, commonly called faculties. Because God is triune, that is three Persons in one, we might think of these faculties of ours as reflecting God's Image in us: the Father, the will; the Son, the reason; the Holy Spirit, the feelings. In any case, it is urgent that you practice enough introspection on your own, untainted by speculation or the "expert," to perceive that among your possessions are three faculties designed as servants of the self: will, mind, feeling. (And, of course, you inhabit a body provided to do your bidding; we will get to that later, when the resurrection is before us).

Keep your relation to these three capacities clear and orderly. None of them is satisfied with serving you. Each can be misled by the Devil into wanting to be master in the house of your self.

Note well that none of these servants is to be confused with the self. Flee every teaching to the contrary. You are not your intellect. You are not your will. You are not your emotions. You are the self, the Image-bearing Person whose servants these faculties are meant to be. To let any one dominate you is to serve it as an idol. You cannot serve God and intellect, nor God and will, nor God and emotion. That is why so many selves stagger as it were drunkenly about, victimized one hour by their feelings, the next hour by their intellect and a third by the will, all the while confusing this with freedom.

Unfortunately, a vast deal of "evangelism," by-passing the Creed, is mis-directed upon making an idol out of the emotions, the feelings of exuberance, the sense of security, while much of theologizing bows to the idol of the intellect, the authority of the "scholar." Tyranny in Church or state exults the will. But the "worship" of idols is strictly God-forbidden: *"You shall have no other gods before me"* (Ex. 20:3). It's you who matters; just God and you and your obedience to Him by way of your faculties.

The Word of God comes from the divine Self to the human self. One-to-one. We are commanded to receive God's Word as from His own lips. Communion with God via that Word is from the divine SELF to the human self, as immediate as from parent to child. God's Word is not to be filtered through intellect, the feeling, nor the will, much as the Devil would like to control that Word through these would-be idols. These servants are indeed given to facilitate our obedience to the divine revelation, but are endowed with no authority to warp the form of believing obedience.

You have to make sure that "I" am in charge here, and responsible to God for my stewardship of His gifts of will, mind and feeling in doing good works to His service.

And now, "believe...."

Believing, the active form of faith, is a crucial term in Christianity. It is, in fact, crucial in life itself. We live by believing, not only as Christians but as human beings. We will explore that a little.

Christian believing is the God-ward side of self-denial. We don't mount to Him. He comes to us, in countless ways and especially in His Word. He enters by way of our believing. Let's just say that when we begin the Creed with "I believe," this is what we mean: we invite the words that follow to take possession of our selves!

Either we want to be servants of what we say we believe, or in fact we do not believe. The Holy Spirit uses the Word He inspires as Light for us to "see" by, and as Power for us to live according to what we see.

In a certain sense, believing is not "act," but the absence of "act." The Church has long compared "believing" to the open mouth of a bottle ready to receive whatever is poured in. We come to Word and to Creed as self-emptied of our own wishes, of our own ideas, of our own schemes and intentions. We wait for Word and Creed to be poured in. All other "gods" are suppressed. We wish to bring nothing but the will to hear. And we know that by "hear" the Bible means to listen with a will to obey.

Long ago, the boy Samuel was being raised in God's temple at Shiloh under the old highpriest Eli. One night Samuel heard his name being called in the dim light shed by a temple lamp. He hastened to Eli, saying, *"Here I am, for you called me."* But the highpriest had not called him. Twice this happened. And then Eli realized that God was calling the lad, and said to him, *"Go, lie down; and if he calls you, you shall say, 'Speak, Lord, for your servant hears.'"* Samuel obeyed, and that is what being God's servant means!

It was indeed God who was calling Samuel, with bad news. He told the boy that the house of Eli was about to fall, thanks to the sins of Eli's two sons. Samuel had to relate this message to Eli in the morning (I Sam. 3:2-14). And his model remains: *"Speak, Lord, for your servant hears!"* Such servants we are to be, always, as we come to Bible, Creed, sermon!

Be sure to reflect upon what that means: speak through Thy Word, for I will to do in the power of the Spirit whatever that Word requires. To believe is to open ourselves to control by Word and Spirit.

What will happen?

Wait and see! It's the excitement of the obedient life.

"I believe" does say something about ourselves. It says that we are learning to depend upon revealed Truth to live by, and for.

Now notice that from the non-believer's point of view, "I believe" says something quite different. It seems to say that we are clinging to a poor, weak, fallible substitute for the surety of science, desperately clutching at the last knot on the end of a fragile, outworn rope which we hope will save us from drowning in the flood of events. That's how the secular mind looks at your "I believe." Don't be intimidated!

Let the modern mind sneer its disdain. Let it jeer at what it calls a useless launching pad into life. Only believe? Next-door neighbor to ignorance? Mere faith? Isn't that what one says when you cannot be sure--I "believe"? Still more, isn't it true that what matters in life is what you know, indeed what you know for sure!

You begin to see, now, what kind of a mirror to who you are the Creed turns out to be for unbelief. The "I believe" shows that you must be adrift upon the ugly sea of history with only faith to cling to. The pseudo-sophisticated jeer, "Better get with science!"

The authority of "science," the certainty of "science," gets dinned into your ears everywhere. Belief cuts a pretty poor figure in the news compared with "science." It is always implied that only the foolish, the ignorant, the simple go in for faith. The intelligent, the really with-it, rest upon the certainties of "science."

Swimming against that current seems almost impossible until you reflect upon a few things so easily overlooked, like:

1. "Science" itself rests upon faith. Yes, upon faith in our senses, faith in the idols of logic, faith in the accuracy of observation, faith in mathematics, and the like. None provable.

2) "Science" is in fact forever in flux, with today's certainty becoming tomorrow's discard. One of the greatest philosophers of science in our century, Alfred North Whitehead, wrote in the 1920s, "The old foundations of scientific thought are becoming unintelligible. Time, space, matter, material, ether, electricity, mechanism, organism, configuration, structure, pattern, function, all require reinterpretation. What is the sense of talking about a mechanical explanation when you don't know what you mean by mechanics?" (Science And The Modern World, p. 16). That is not less true, but more so, now, than when Whitehead made the observation.

3) It all comes down to whose "word" governs your acts, God's or man's. God's Word affords us the only absolute source of certainty available to mankind. "Science" always falls short of its claims.

The so-called "certainties" of "science" rest upon what might be called a "natural faith." And people are indeed dependent upon it before we even know that it exists.

The natural faith of daily life is the wager we must make to keep the wheels of society in motion, and it always leaves us with a margin of error.

We have no practical option, for example, but to believe the reports of our senses, and to act upon them. We must believe that what we think we see is really there. We must believe that what we think we hear is accurate, etc. In short, we must believe reports of our senses, even though we know by experience that their reports can be wayward and play us false. We must, further, believe our memories; we have to believe that how we reason is trustworthy, that our logic holds good and that figures don't lie--even though all of these forms of faith have sometimes misled us.

So in fact "science" appeals to belief, just as does the Creed. It's not a matter of know for "science," versus believe for religious faith. Max Planck, originator of the ruling "quantum mechanics," writes: "...over the entrance to the gates of the temple of science are written the words: Ye must have faith" (Where Is Science Going?, p. 214). It's forever a simple choice: whose word do I believe? That's all.

So, look carefully about you.

Recognize that without natural faith, both personal and communal living is impossible. As already noted, our whole lives are environed by natural faith, yet never yielding us absolute certainty. We may add that we must also believe in the general regularities of nature, in the probability of normal behavior by others, in the stability of our institutions, in the keeping of promises, in the relatively enduring worth of money, and on and on. So much do we live by natural faith as to be shocked or annoyed when things, or people, don't behave as we unconsciously believed they would, or should.

It's only those who fail to acknowledge the role of natural faith in everyday life who fall into caricature of religious faith as the fragile last resort of a beaten spirit. They portray reliance upon belief as implying a frightening vulnerability to, say, the assault of science and skepticism. They foolishly caricature Christianity as thriving on "mere" faith, as hinged upon "mere" believing, motivated by fear. All the time they themselves are totally dependent upon natural faith for existence.

Take careful note that it is not "science" which certifies a confident "I know" in the face of life. Scientific certainty is always within a range of probability, plus or minus some percent. Yet you as believer thrive in the astonishing paradox that your seemingly fragile "I believe" admits the indestructible, Word-validated certainty of "I know!" Something which unbelief never understands.

Our "I believe" is not a clutching at straws in the wild seas of life, while "science" or philosophy or common sense is so much more secure. The believer's experience reveals just the opposite.

The Word which enters via "I believe" environs you in the only absolute certainty any human can ever enjoy. How else could it be, when the Word on which faith thrives is that of God the Father Almighty! And when our conviction that the Word speaks true is created by God the Holy Spirit!

Jesus, you know, often concluded an act of healing by saying, *"Your faith has made you whole"* (as in Mat. 9:22; Mark 5:34; Luke 8:48, etc.). Here He reveals the very essence of believing. The act of faith, that is of believing, simply opened the believer to the power of the Lord's Word. Faith "makes whole" by opening the self to the whole-making Word. Jesus can say, "Your faith has made you whole" because His healing Word comes in via our believing.

"I know," says Job, with his world in ruins about him, *"that my Redeemer lives, and at last he will stand upon the earth; and after my skin has been thus destroyed, then from my flesh I shall see God, whom I shall see on my side, and my eyes shall behold, and not another"* (Job 19:25). Notice that: I know! Whence had Job such certainty, looking clear-eyed through the temporal to see in it the witness to the eternal? Job had lost all that was most precious to him. How did he know that, despite all appearances, his Redeemer lives? By faith! His faith, like yours, admits certainty.

Again, there is St. Paul: *"...for I know whom I have believed, and I am persuaded that he is able to keep until that Day what has been entrusted to me"* (II Tim. 1:12). "I know" and "am persuaded...." The fruit of faith; the certainty the Spirit creates within. How frail and weak by comparison are the 'certainties' based upon science.

Yes, it is one of God's judgments on arrogance to provide our "I believe" with absolute certainty, while to unbelief "science" seems so secure and faith so tentative. Is God perhaps a little amused by the bluster of skepticism? That is, until the Day of Judgment.

The Bible offers us a familiar definition of believing or faith: *"Now faith is the substance of things hoped for, the evidence of things not seen"* (Heb. 11:1). It's a comforting and illumining revelation. Think on it.

Believing, that is faith, lends substance, that is <u>gives existence in our experience</u>, to the hopes spun off by God's Word. Hopes like assurance of life eternal, joy, peace, trust, certainty, strength, courage, fidelity--all get a reality, a substance, as they pass through faith from the Word into our lives. Something happens via faith. Meaning becomes substantial. Take for example:

"Peace I leave with you," Jesus says, *"my peace I give you"* (John 14:27). Do we know what He means? Yes, we do. But there is more. We actually experience the substance of His promise. Peace becomes ours. We have His Word, heard in faith, as the reality of our experience. His Word "peace" becomes our reality, thanks to the gift of faith. He says, "<u>I give;</u>" by faith we have. Consider that promise; savor it; expect to feel it as a balm for all the tensions of the day. <u>Because</u> faith <u>is</u> the substance of things hoped for!

Again, Jesus says, *"And I will pray the Father, and he will give you another Counselor, to be with you forever, even the Spirit of truth, whom the world cannot receive, because it neither sees him nor knows him; you know him, for he dwells with you, and will be in you"* (John 14:16-17). We will recall this promise when we come to our confession of belief in the Holy Spirit through Article 8 of the Creed. Through faith we experience the substance of that Gift.

And this matter of "evidence of things not seen:" Our "I believe" can be sluggish, laggard, falling behind our needs in the hurly-burly of life. But if we nourish it on the Word, and persevere, our believing will indeed become evidence of the divine power, divine initiative and enthusiasm blazing out of the Word through the agency of the Holy Spirit.

In times of confrontation--"how do you know?"--in times of self-doubt--"how can I be sure?" God's Word received in faith becomes evidence we live on without knowing how it occurs. O keep your Bible ever close at hand.

Never, never be talked out of reliance upon "I believe." Never, never hope to find greater certainty in some other way. Through the "I believe" we ordinary people become companions of God along the ways of life. For faith is the substance of things hoped for, and faith <u>is</u> the evidence of things not seen. It's certified in the crucible of experience, by the testimony of those who suffer for their "I believe," even of martyrs who give their lives for the "evidence of things not seen" by their persecutors.

There is no more creative, romantic, optimistic vision of human and cosmic history than that opened to faith by Christianity. It's just because our faith is indeed substance and evidence of the active presence of God in every event that occupies our lives. He is there! Not only that, but He governs, He is in control, and He is in Jesus Christ our loving and indulgent Father, and through the Spirit He endows our days with peace, strength, and joy.

God as Father so governs the moments of time that the tangled skein of our so-botched lives comes out to our advantage, even when we don't quite get the point ourselves.

"We know," Paul tells us, *"that in everything God works for good with those who love him, who are called according to his purpose. "*

And now follows the revelation of our predestination: *"For those whom he fore-knew he also predestined to be conformed to the image of his Son, in order that he might be first-born among many within a large family. And those whom he pre-destined he also called; and those whom he called he also justified; and those whom he justified he also glorified. What then shall we say to this? If God is for us, who is against us? He who did not spare his own Son but gave him up for us all, will he not also give us all things with him?"*

And then the transcendent conclusion: *"For I am sure that neither death, nor life, nor angels, nor principalities, nor things present, nor things to come, nor powers, nor height, nor depth, nor anything else in all creation, will be able to separate us from the love of God in Christ Jesus our Lord"* (Rom. 8:28-32; 37-39).

All this, through faith, becomes substantial reality in our experience, guides us through the days and nights, and serves as evidence for all the blessing that lies ahead. The Word is the substance; the Word is the evidence. And we are the beneficiaries of the inexhaustible resources come to hand in Truth received through faith.

Let unbelief scoff; let the secular mind demean; let the arrogant sneer. Know that your "I believe" opens to the only absolute substance, the only unassailable evidence to be found in the great universe hung before us as witness to the power and majesty of God the Father, maker of heaven and earth.

Is "I believe" all we have for such certainty? Yes, and more than enough! Rejoice in the gift of faith; live in and through it; exploit it; revel in it. Thank God you can say, "I believe...!"

It is His gift.

It's a little term, this "in." We could pass it by, except that it performs a crucial function. The "in" points to the mysterious union of God and believer by way of faith. God comes "in" via Word and Spirit through the access provided by believing. Just how Word and Spirit enter as it were from afar, and just how, hearing the Word we live in the light of the very precincts of heaven, we cannot explain. But as believer you can know!

"Of course, I believe that God exists," can be glibly mouthed by anyone. It may come as an aside, a concession, a discovery, treating God as just one other among existents. Just as one says that there is another side to the moon.

But the Creed carefully avoids having us say, "I believe that...." Why?

Because a "that" would be our work, our discovery, our inference. But "in" is His doing. Still more, to believe only that God exists equates us with devils. St. James says sardonically: *"You believe that God is one; you do well. Even demons believe--and tremble"* (James 2:19).

We may say that the "in" is there to highlight the believer's experience. Via His Word received through faith, God the Holy Spirit indeed does come "in." That is, God and Word act as one, when the Word is received by faith.

Through believing we enter "in"-to a relationship unlike any other. "In" God, you are forever validated, established, accepted, as person. You need seek no other vindication of existence.

Jesus graphically describes how He, as the divine Word, seeks the faith which gives the Word entry: *"Behold, I stand at the door, knocking; if you hear my voice and open the door, I will come in to you and eat with you, and you with me"* (Rev. 3:20). Jesus knocks by way of His voice as recorded in the Scriptures and preached from the faithful pulpit. His "voice" conveys His Word. Indeed, He Himself comes as Word. You need not try to imagine a "personal" relationship with Him. The Word which is received through faith is the very living presence of the Master. *"The words that I have spoken to you,"* he says to His disciples, *"are spirit and life"* (John 6:63).

Via the Word He comes "in." We thus say, "I believe in...." as we open ourselves to words that follow in the Creed and all that they mean to our daily living.

The "in" anchors the self, anchors you, in the only absolute security we can find, and the only confirmation of our worth that we need.

Through believing "in" God, we open ourselves to the ultimate confirmation of self-worth implied by our possession of God's Image. Neither counselor, nor guru, nor training course in assertive practices, nor psychiatrist's couch can provide the certainty of self-worth open to faith out of the Word through which God Himself comes "in" to overcome self-doubt, anxiety, despair. No other relation can do that. You, as Image-bearing believer, can find "in" the power of the Image-Giver all the self-assurance required for walking with confidence the life of priestly obedience in the world.

Neither Freud, nor Jung, nor Adler nor any other "doctor of the soul" is needed for walking tall in the world, whatever be your status in society, when believing "in" God environs the self. Because the believer is "in" believing relationship with God, we need seek no other proofs of worth, nor guarantees of value. Nor can we find them elsewhere than in the Word.

The little "in" carries a lot of blessing, then, when recognized as pointing to that relation between God and you which undergirds your life with the only genuine confidence in self and future which is given to mankind. God is "for" you and "in" you, even as we all are in Him. Let us rejoice "in" that.

With what is so commonly called your own "self-image" anchored securely "in" God through faith "in" His Word, you have no right to be concerned with how your "self" appears to others. What matters is how you appear to God. And how you appear to God is directly proportional to your receipt of His word through faith, and your striving for obedience to it.

We are "in" God. Life is given to behave like it.

What is to be said about God here?

What could be even remotely adequate?

We will shortly repeat what the Creed places on our lips about Him, "the Father almighty, maker of heaven and earth...."

We will rehearse what this Father has done and does for our restoration of communion with Himself which is life, now and forever. That's what the Creed summarizes for us.

But of God Himself, what is to be said?

Far better, John Calvin advises, than trying to speculate about the being and nature of God, let us seek after His revelation of how He wishes us to relate to Him, and what He does to make that possible.

We can, though, repeat what one of the greatest of the Prophets says to us, and for us, about God.

Let's do so, next:

"To whom will you compare me, that I should be like him? says the Holy One. Lift up your eyes on high and see: who created these? He who brings out their host by number, calling them all by name; By the greatness of his might, and because he is strong in power, not one is missing. Why do you say, O Jacob, and speak, O Israel, 'My way is hid from the Lord, and my right is disregarded by my God'? Have you not known? Have you not heard? The Lord is the everlasting God, the Creator of the ends of the earth. He does not grow faint or grow weary, his under-standing is unsearchable. He gives power to the faint, and to him who has no might, he increases strength. Even youths shall faint and be weary, and young men shall fall exhausted; but they who wait upon the Lord shall renew their strength, they shall mount up with wings like eagles, they shall run and not be weary, they shall walk and not faint." (Is. 40:25-31).

You see how the prophet moves from the majestic reality of God to the blessing which this confers upon us who believe, illustrating Calvin's advice that it is far better to think on how God relates to us than to speculate upon who and what God in Himself can be. We are, by faith in the living God, as Paul tells us, *"more than conquerors through him who loved us"* (Rom. 8:37).

So, then, let it be: I BELIEVE IN GOD...!!!

We discover that we do come to "know" God in the experience of what are commonly called His attributes. No, it's not just saying these terms; it's not even defining what they mean. Experience them! Be aware of God acting everywhere in these ways:

1. God is <u>omnipresent</u> and <u>omniscient,</u> everywhere and everywhen present, and all-knowing. We have already noted St. Paul's saying (Acts 17:28) that *"in him we live and move and have our being."* The Psalmist says the same: *"O Lord, you have searched me and known me. You know when I sit down and when I rise up; you discern my thoughts from far away. You search out my path and my lying down, and are acquainted with all my ways. Even before a word is on my tongue, O Lord, you know it completely. You hem me in, behind and before, and lay your hand upon me. Such knowledge is too wonderful for me; it is so high that I cannot attain it"* (Ps. 139:1-6). "Too wonderful," indeed, for us to lay hold of through the servant intellect. But, as the Psalmist testifies, we know God's omniscient omnipresence through the experience of its reality. God's self-definition as *"I AM"* (Ex. 3:14) means ever, and always, and everywhere THERE, HERE, NOW! To experience this omnipresence is "knowing" God, and, finding in that knowledge an enduring foundation of security, a key to walking tall as His child in His world.

Knowing God is becoming aware, always becoming more aware, of His omniscience! Nothing we do that He does not see; nothing we think that He does not hear; nothing we are that He does not know: *"Understand, O dullest of the people! Fools, when will you be wise? He who planted the ear, does he not hear? He who formed the eye, does he not see?"* (Ps. 94:8-9). For the believer, the source of utmost comfort and fortitude! For the non-believer, subtle discomfort and hardly conscious awareness of impending judgment.

The Bible keeps tuned to God as omnipresent: *"Whither shall I go from your Spirit? Or whither shall I flee from your presence? If I ascend to heaven, you are there! If I make my bed in Sheol, you are there! If I take the wings of the morning and dwell in the uttermost parts of the sea, even there your hand shall lead me, and your right hand shall hold me. If I say, 'Surely the darkness shall cover me, and the light around me become night,' even darkness is not dark to you; the night is as bright as day, for darkness is as light to you"* (Ps. 139:7-12).

How deeply at odds, this, with the secular mind of our times. God in every nook and cranny of our selves, of our world, of our behavior! God immediately aware of how we treat every facet of His world: is there a more compelling ground for a true environmentalism? And there is God taking note of how all of His creatures behave toward each other: could there be a more powerful incentive for justice, personal and social?

God's attributes are those of a Person. We know a Him, not an It, in the experience of His ever present, all-knowing Self.

We may speak of gravity as the force that keeps things on earth from flying off in all directions, the force that brings us tumbling down if we slip and fall. But gravity knows nothing about its effects. It is force, indeed force sustained by God, but wholly impersonal. God is ever present, that is omnipresent, as Person, aware of all that He makes happen. He is all-knowing, omniscient. In His knowing all things, He is 'there' as they occur.

Recognizing that God knows all that we think, say and do underlies the witness of conscience in our lives. Conscience comes with His Image. It implies a knowing-with, (con:with; science:knowledge). "So conscience doth make cowards of us all," Shakespeare says. It is, indeed, so mysterious a voice that great efforts are made by some to deny its reality. Your conscience is God-given witness to the omnipresent omniscience of Him who makes and sustains, and loves, us.

We can find in conscience a resource in one problematic situation after another. The voice is there. The better we know the Word of God the more precise are the verdicts of conscience. And conscience can make stalwarts of those who know that God knows all. The ever-present God is the all-knowing God.

3. God is also omnipotent, all-powerful. The tides of life may break over the Rock upon whom our faith rests, but cannot dislodge us. In the favorite Psalm of Oliver Cromwell, the 46th, David writes, *"God is our refuge and strength, a very present help in trouble. Therefore we will not fear though the earth be removed, and though the mountains be carried into the midst of the sea; though the waters thereof roar and be troubled, though the mountains shake with the swelling thereof"* (Ps. 46:1-3).

When the disciples of Jesus were storm-tossed one night on the sea of Galilee, He comes to them walking on the writhing waters, and calls out: *"Take heart, it is I; have no fear"* (Mark 6:50). And as He enters their boat, the sea is becalmed. So, on another occasion when He stilled the raging waves, the disciples ask themselves, *"Who then is this, that he commands even wind and water, and they obey him?"* (Luke 8:25). So, of course, He comes to us via His Word when life tosses us about and fear haunts our hearts. He expels fear because we know Him to be omnipresent, omniscient, omnipotent.

Thus we "know" God in the very experience of His attributes, and in reflection upon such experience. And we come better and better to understand what St. Paul means by writing to us, and for us, of God that He *"is able to do far more abundantly than all that we ask or think"* (Eph. 3:20). Rejoice!

Let us sum up schematically, in anticipation of what follows in the Creed, what we are now going to confess. We will use an IF...THEN formula.

1) **IF** there is a God, **THEN** how does He stand over against us?

The Creed's answer: as "Father!"

Muse on it! Think on it! Rejoice in it! Bask in it!

God is twice, in fact, our Father, once by our creation into life natural, and again by our redemption through His Son into life super-natural.

2) **IF** God reveals Himself as our Father, **THEN** what is His status relative to other powers in the universe? Are there malignant forces more powerful? demons able to elude His reach? natural laws to which He must bow? systems He has set in motion from which He is then excluded, as in evolutionary theories?

The Creed's answer: "The Father" is "almighty!" He coerces all, and is coerced by nothing. He is ruler of all, and ruled by no one and no-thing.

3) **IF** God is Almighty Father, **THEN** what display of that omnipotence does He set ever before us?

The Creed's answer: God the Father Almighty is "maker of heaven and earth," with ourselves included. *"It is he who made us, and not we ourselves"* (Ps. 100:3).

4) **IF** God is all this for us, **THEN** what profit have we in it?

The Creed's answer: God *"gave his only Son, that whoever believes in him should not perish but have eternal life"* (John 3:16). And so we go on to gain ever more from that glorious revelation along the route laid out by the Creed.

Before we confess God as Creator, we confess Him as Father. It is not as Force, nor as Bang, nor as irresistible energy that God creates. He creates as Person, the original and eternal SELF, willing to be known to believers as Father because He is in fact Father to all creation.

One Father, one family!

God the Father surely made the cosmos to be, as it were, a playhouse for His Image-bearing children, in size and complexity a fit counterpart and infinite challenge to the implanted potential of His own Image. The limitless extent and variety of the creation, of which in fact we understand so little, advertises the anticipations the Father had for His Image-bearing offspring--and has still for those who by faith *"wait for new heavens and a new earth in which righteousness dwells"* (II Pet. 3:13).

But now, thanks to the event called the "Fall," we are limited to poor, restricted hazardous explorations of a universe designed by our Father for our delight.

Space exploration goes on apace. A marvel? Yes, and witness to divinely implanted human ingenuity and courage, too. But, when the secular mind boasts in human achievement, the believer reflects on how paltry are those best efforts for a creature made in the Image of God and destined to rove the universe! God made for man the farthest stars. It was a status man forfeited in the first rebellion in the Garden of Eden. It will come again anew!

"For eye has not seen, nor ear heard, nor the heart of man conceived, what God has prepared for those who love him" (I Cor. 2:9, quoting Is. 64:4; 65:7).

The family serves as foundation of society. And Father implies family. God is *"...the Father,"* writes Paul, *"from whom every family in heaven and earth is named"* (Eph. 3:15).

The human family is anchored in God as Father, with the human mother as clearly the "heart" of the home as the father is its "head," and the Bible requires the obedience of the child to both: *"Honor your father and your mother, as the Lord your God commanded you, that your days may be prolonged, and that it may go well with you in the land which the Lord your God gives you"* (Deut. 5:16). *"This is,"* Paul writes, *"the first commandment with a promise"* (Eph. 6:2). How serious this command is, and how devastating is its violation, is apparent everywhere as the family disintegrates. The Fatherhood of God imposes the pattern of the family upon parents and children. Destruction of the family inevitably entails corruption of society itself.

How ultimately devastating a mistake it is to suppose, as is too commonly done, that there can be any substitute for the family in the life of the growing child. Neither school, nor counselor, nor baby-sitter, nor mountains of toys can substitute for the home where father and mother play their indispensable roles in the rearing of the young. The mother who pursues, and the father who concurs in the wife's exchange of a job for full-time motherhood invites grave ultimate consequences whatever material gains, or elevation of social status, may be in view.

Maintenance of the inviolability of the family should be social priority number one. Would that many of the billions of dollars dribbled away behind the facade of "education" were directed upon the support of families, and that the accolades paid "successful" women in business affairs were addressed to enhancing motherhood.

The family is not the product of social evolution. The revelation of God as "the Father" stamps the human family as His creation. It is His choice of fundamental means to ensure the social health of mankind. It is implied in our confession of Him as Father.

Because God reveals Himself as Father, Jesus can require of each of us a re-ordering of secular values: *"Therefore, I tell you, do not be anxious about your life, what you shall eat or what you shall drink, nor about your body, what you shall put on....saying, 'What shall we eat?' or, 'What shall we drink?' or 'What shall we wear?' For the Gentiles seek all these things; and your heavenly Father knows that you need them all. But seek first his kingdom and his righteousness, and all these things shall be yours as well"* (Mat. 6:25,31-33).

"The Gentiles" is the Lord's term here for victims of unbelief. The believer is relieved by God, because He is our Father, from the secular mind's over-riding worries. Living in this Light becomes a test of our faith, one that will meet us often and one which we can pass only with the internal aid of the Spirit.

Paul stresses the same point: *"There is great gain in godliness with contentment; for we brought nothing into this world, and it is certain that we can take nothing out; but if we have food and clothing, with these we shall be content. But those who desire to be rich fall into temptation, into a snare, into many senseless and hurtful desires that plunge men into ruin and destruction. For the love of money is the root of all evils... "* (I Tim. 6:6-10).

Are we "fussed and fagged," as the poet Hopkins puts it, about daily cares? Ask, then, do we really know God as Father? Do we truly trust the Word of our Lord? These pivotal questions are easier asked than answered in the affirmative. Who does not fall far short of perfect faith? But, we are indeed instructed not to be anxious about the so-called necessities of life, because we have a heavenly Father who knows all about such needs and will satisfy them according to His own prescription of our best interests. It is a goal to strive for by prayer and recourse to His Word. Liberation from material concerns frees us, Jesus says, to be sure that God's Word governs our behavior as we go about our own work in the world.

It is the language of our prayer: Thy kingdom come, Thy will be done, on earth...!

In short, when we confess believing in God the Father almighty, we imply obedience to Jesus' command that we expend no concern over the worries of the "Gentiles." For if we do that, then we contradict our own confession of faith in God as Father. What we claim by confession to believe has a way of doubling back for testing by our behavior. Keep an eye open for that.

This is a religious, not a philosophical, confession. Nothing implied here, therefore, of the tantalizing puzzles about irresistible force and immovable object, etc. That is for speculation. The Creed is for life. Here all is light, and in it we are permitted to see God the Father as:

<u>Almighty</u>: competent to our every need, those which we know and (even more assuring) those known only to Him. Nothing beyond the range of His observation, beyond the scope of His power.

<u>Almighty</u>: absolute superiority to all enemies including death itself: *"The last enemy to be destroyed is death"* (I Cor. 15:26). The Almighty is on our side, not the enemy's, nor is He neutral.

<u>Almighty</u>: in the salvation of all who believe, with divine provision also for the restoration of heaven and earth: *"...because the creation itself will be set free from its bondage to decay and obtain the glorious liberty of the children of God"* (Rom. 8:21).

<u>Almighty</u>: source of a pervasive sense of blessing: *"All things work together for good for those who love him"* (Rom. 8:28). A power that ranges from the farthest stars to the smallest detail: *"But even the hairs of your head are all numbered,"* Jesus assures us (Mat. 10:30). God's almighty hand is active in our birth and life-long: *"Before I formed you in the womb,"* God says to the Prophet Jeremiah, *"I knew you, and before you were born I consecrated you"* (Jer. 1:5). Of course revealed so that we too may know that God superintended our conception and birth, and after birth: *"My times are in thy hand"* (Ps. 31:15).

<u>Almighty</u>: our very ability to say "I believe" testifies to the Father's love and almighty care: *"Even as He chose us in him [Jesus Christ] before the foundation of the world, that we should be holy and blameless before Him"* (Eph. 1:4).

Because God is almighty, <u>therefore</u> He CAN provide whatever is necessary for our temporal and eternal welfare. <u>Because</u> God is Father, <u>therefore</u> He WILL do so for all whose "I believe" truly opens them to the Power of the Spirit and Light of the Word.

The revelation of divine sovereignty, that God the Father is <u>almighty</u> raises problems, very ancient ones.

We must face them, come to decision and move on.

Because God reveals Himself as almighty, then:

A. What about human free will? Who but God can be free in a universe where His will is omnipotent? But, does not this imply a kind of fatalism?

B. What, then, about human responsibility? Can God demand obedience to His Law, as He clearly does, and hold man responsible for sin and evil, if all the while God is in absolute control of human behavior? Not, then, "the Devil made me do it," but "God made me do it"? Is this not implied by "almighty"?

C. What about the Last Judgment? What can God judge man for on that Last Day if all things have ever been under His absolute control?

And yet the Bible, and especially the Lord Jesus, point unmistakably to a Day of Judgment, that *"great and terrible day of the Lord... "* (Joel 2:31). Jesus says, *"For the Son of man is to come with his angels in the glory of his Father, and then he will repay every one for what he has done"* (Mat. 16:27). Notice: not what "God has done through you" but what "you" have done.

You have but one choice here. It is really just a replay of the alternatives always before us: whose Word? Quite simply, what does the Bible say? That is normative, and it is final. Evasions of the Word will not serve the life of obedience. You just have to read the Book for yourself, and obey.

God is Sovereign. So it is revealed: *"Yours, O Lord, is the greatness, and the power, and the glory and the victory, and the majesty: for all that is in heaven and earth is thine. Thine is the kingdom, O Lord, and thou art exalted as head above all. Both riches and honor come of thee, and thou reignest over all"* (I Chron. 29:11-12).

"He does according to his will, in the army of heaven, and among the inhabitants of the earth: and none can stay his hand, or say unto him, What dost thou?" (Dan. 4:35).

It is a common biblical theme: *"For God is the king of all the earth... God reigns over the nations"* (Ps. 47:7-8). And Jesus Himself, preparing to ascend to His Father's side, says, *"All authority in heaven and on earth has been given to me"* (Mat. 28:18). God is sovereign. Rejoice in it!

Happily say it again: God is sovereign, no doubt about that. The Bible is full of illustrations of divine government of man and world. That is why the Creed obliges us to say, "the Father almighty." Not our discovery. Not the verdict of science or of scholarship. Just plain, simple revelation.

And yet, revelation is equally insistent that we are held fully responsible, each for his own behavior.

"And the dead were judged by what was written in the books, by what they had done" (Rev. 20:12).

"For he will render to every one according to his works..." (Rom. 2:6).

We have heard Jesus Himself foretelling judgment: *"For the Son of man is to come with his angels in the glory of his Father, and then he will repay every one for what he has done"* (Mat. 16:27).

The Bible speaks, clearly and unequivocally:

1) God is absolute Sovereign; and, 2) we, believer and unbeliever alike, are so wholly responsible that final judgment will rest upon our behavior.

We have no choice, really: we live in the light of both the truth of divine Sovereignty and the truth of human responsibility!

Therefore, repeat: 1) God the Father is our sovereign Lord; 2) we are His fully responsible children.

So we are back once more to biblical paradox. Two contradictories are both true: divine sovereignty and human responsibility.

Here, of course, secular unbelief and Christian believing part company. Or, better, God parts them, because it is His Word that rules the believer's perception of life and its circumstances.

The secular mind charges that here the Bible is hopelessly self-contradictory and, therefore, unworthy of belief. A convenient "out" from obligation, bowing before intellect and its logic.

But the believer discovers that because the inspired Word rules both thinking and behavior, mere logic takes its servant's place, grumble as it will. Belief serves the Word; unbelief the idol of the intellect.

What is most useful to us about the great truth of God's sovereignty is the Light in which it will bathe every moment of our lives as we more and more are grasped by its reality. It's not something that comes all at once. The more we mature in the exercise of faith, the more clearly do we "see" that deep down inside all our experience is the presence and power and love of God. Not only as power but no less as Person, not only something but Someone. And you know what "person" means because, being made in His Image, you know what a person is, mystery and all.

And, an interesting thing, every time you become aware that God as living Person is actively at hand in whatever is happening right now, you discover that the fleeting moment of time is offset by the stability of the Now! The Danish philosopher Kierkegaard called it "the moment."

You've never paused to reflect upon what "now" is?

The German philosopher Hegel takes note of it, as do many others. By the time you can say "now," Hegel says in his Phenomenology Of Mind, it is already not-now. Try it. You say "now" and as the sound dies away, it is already "then." The elusive "now" slips by as we try to fasten on it. But, life is made up of "nows." And so, on reflection, living seems to be only a succession of nothings.

But of course our inability to halt time in its tracks does not make living unreal. Rather it teaches us to "see" that the fleeting moments come as God's invitation to observe His presence in and behind time. Time passes; life hastens on; but God is ever right here and now, and invites us to use the moments to experience that and serve Him sacramentally.

Recall that one of the facets of God's warning to Adam and Eve not to eat of the forbidden fruit was that if they ate they would *"surely die"* (Gen. 2:17). They disobeyed. They ate. And they fell out of life in the ever-present Now of the experience of God. They fell into the time, the ever-vanishing Now, the threat of death. Time's flying is inescapable proof of our mortality as descendants of Adam and Eve. Sensitive souls, given to self-expression in the arts and philosophy, have suffered keenly the evanescence of life, to say of each moment with Goethe's Faust, "Stay, thou art so fair!"

But moments have ways of their own. They will not be tamed at our command. God wills it so, a constant reminder that we are heritors of the Fall. We are on our way, no stopping time, to ultimate Destiny, life with or death without communion with God.

The moment flees. They ever will. But God's willingness to have us use moments for communion with Himself, "the everlasting NOW," nullifies the effect of the Fall. His means to this end is the Word.

His Word cuts across the flow of time to set a Rock under our feet in the swift flight of moments. That is the meaning of the call, *"Today, if you will hear his voice, harden not your hearts..."* (Ps. 95:7, quoted Heb. 3:7). It is always a "today" in the midst of the swift passage of our "nows." It is always opportunity. If you did not hear a moment ago, listen now!

The passing moment is not only witness to our want, to our depravity, but much more witness to His sufficiency. He speaks now! He is ever speaking now, and calling us to hear and obey. That's the Rock firm-standing against the floods of time.

Let us always remember to discern in every event of the day the active presence of God. He infuses all history with his superintending providence. Much is mysterious; much beyond our ken. But we enter the Kingdom of Heaven, not only in doing good works, not only in praise and worship, but also in seeking to acknowledge God's hand in the stuff of the day, like the glory of the sunrise, the placidity of the moon-light, the joy of loving companionship, the thrill of achievement, the peace of faith. He shapes our ends, rough-hew them as we will, as Shakespeare says.

To know Him thus is foretaste of life eternal.

Consider each "now" given you as opportunity. And use as many of them as you can for letting God freeze the flow of time in the experience of His Word.

Received by faith, and enlivened by the Spirit, the Word infuses us with life in the very midst of death-dealing time. Let phrases and sentences recalled from the Bible occupy your thoughts as the days pass swiftly by. *"The Lord is my shepherd...."* (Ps. 23:1). *"He will give his angels charge of you...."* (Ps. 91:11). The Psalms have ever been found by believers across the ages an inexhaustible trove of Words composed to lift the heart, open the inner eye, charm the inner ear, soothe the soul, fortify the will, bind up wounds. The Psalms, Calvin teaches, are given for the very purpose of putting in our souls and upon our lips praise of God in His own inspired language. Use them that way! Plus using all the resources of the whole Bible to make a "now" into a building block of character.

It's a clear test, useful to face thus early in the Creed: do you rejoice in the light of divine sovereignty as you pursue the life of obedience? Or do you flinch before the scorn of unbelief at your acceptance of paradox, that is God's absolute governance and our absolute responsibility?

Happily for us, the Bible itself blends paradox into one harmonious whole, which the believer finds precisely fits experience.

Hear once again the inspired Word through St. Paul: *"Therefore, my beloved, as you have always obeyed, so now, not only as in my presence but much more in my absence, work out your own salvation with fear and trembling; for God is at work in you, both to will and to work for his good pleasure"* (Phil. 2:12-13). Think on it: 1) you must *"work out"* because 2) *"God is at work in you. "*

Do they fit? No, not logically, but perfectly in our search for the life of obedience.

"Work out your own salvation"--yes, of course, such commitment to obedience is clearly implied by my "I believe." It parallels our Lord's command to, *"Seek first the kingdom... "* (Mat. 6:33). That is the Christian life. It's our dedication to what we are taught to pray for, *"Thy kingdom come, Thy will be done, on earth!"* To seek the life of obedience is what it's all about: *"Let your light so shine before men, that they may see your good works and give glory to your Father in heaven"* (Mat. 5:16).

And, praise God, in making the effort, day by day, we are refreshed to hear the Scripture say, *"For God is at work in you... both to will and to do"*--the only way we could hope to make it.

For logic, our logic, unmanageable. What an irresistible opportunity for unbelief to reject obedience. Hear the sneering, "God asking us to forego logic? No self-respecting person...etc.!" How easy. And how common.

But for us who speak the Creed, just another illustration of how unwise it is to depend upon the dictates of the servant intellect. In the life of the believer, there is perfect harmony between 1) God my Father in absolute control, and 2) my striving daily to act like His disciple knowing that He holds me accountable for success. Exactly! What would I accomplish were it not for the indwelling power of the Spirit? What, indeed, are my best efforts but *"the fruit of the Spirit"* (Gal. 5:22-23)? But what "fruits" unless I do them?

So it is written!!

Well, there is another bone of contention, a correlative and familiar problem, urged by the idol intellect against the revelation that God is almighty. It involves divine predestination.

Some obviously have faith. Some don't. The number around the strait gate onto the narrow way is sparse; the mob around the wide gate onto the broad way is enormous. So Jesus says (Mat. 7:13-14). It's His Word, not that of some myopic theologian, some supposedly mankind-hating John Calvin. Why that difference?

And how are those contrasting numbers related to the divine sovereignty and human responsibility we have been thinking about? How related both to the gift of faith and to its absence? If faith is God's gift, why is it not provided equally to all? If faith is given to the "elect" but denied to the "reprobate," then what of ultimate responsibility? Might God be accountable in some sense for those damned in the last judgment?--a question only blasphemy can entertain seriously.

Again: what does the Bible say?

Divine election:

"We know," as the Spirit reveals through St. Paul, *"that in everything God works for good with those who love him, who are called according to his purpose. For those whom he foreknew he also predestined to the image of his Son, in order that he might be the first-born in a large family. And those whom he predestined he also called; and those he called he also justified; and those whom he justified he also glorified"* (Rom. 8:28-30).

Again, Paul teaches, *"...even as he chose us in him [Christ Jesus] before the foundation of the world, that we should be holy and blameless before him"* (Eph. 1:4). And, further in the same chapter, why He so chose us: *"For we are his workmanship, created in Christ Jesus for good works, which God prepared beforehand, that we should walk in them"* (Eph. 1:10).

Believers are "elected." No doubt of that. But elected to what? To an easy trip to heaven? To a free pass to choice celestial accommodations?

No, divine election is simply appointment, here and now, to walking the narrow road of good works! That is, we are elected to priestly citizenship in the Kingdom of Heaven on earth! *"Thus you will know them,"* Jesus says, *"by their fruits"* (Mat. 7:20). Election shows!

And what of those who choose the broad way to destruction?

What, then, of those crowding the broad way to destruction? Is not the daily news often about their misdeeds?

By our logic, if God chose certain ones to citizenship in His kingdom in time and for eternity, then God at the same time cast aside those not so selected. But we have learned to be cautious about declarations emanating from our intellect. Let us not try to lay down logical consequences to the Sovereign Lord.

Again, our only resource has to be what the Bible reveals.

First, we turn to that section in the book of Romans (9-11) where Paul deals with the Jews' rejection of Jesus as Messiah. As St. John reports it, *"He came unto his own, and his own received him not"* (John 1:11). Why was that? What role did divine sovereignty play in it?

Paul recalls the history of early Israel. When Isaac's wife Rebecca conceived twins, Esau and Jacob, *"Though they were not yet born and had done nothing either good or bad, in order that God's purpose of election might continue, not because of works but because of his call, she was told, 'The elder will serve the younger.' As it is written [in Malachi 1:2-3] 'Jacob have I loved, but Esau I hated'"* (Rom. 9:11-13). Esau was born first, but did not get the birthright--by divine foreordination. So Paul says. The story is told in Genesis, chapters 25-27.

Paul concludes: *"So then he has mercy upon whomever he wills, and he hardens the heart of whomever he wills"* (Rom. 9:18).

"Our God is in the heavens; he does what he pleases" (Ps. 115:3).

The Bible sets the ultimate destiny of every human being within divine sovereignty. And so, St. Paul can phrase the skeptic's question for him: "Is there injustice on God's part?" That's the choice our idol intellect would set before us. And how readily the secular mind, serving that idol, responds with hearty affirmation: "Sure is!"

But not so the Apostle: *"By no means! Let God be true though everyone a liar"* (Rom. 3:4).

Make no mistake. You are to choose the teaching of the Word, not the verdict of any other source, including your intellect.

Think not to appeal to logic, to other authority, to your own sense of fair play. There is only one tribunal in these high matters. It is the inspired Word of God. Hear it! Deny your self, and obey.

God is Sovereign. Also in lives of unbelief.

The Bible clearly reveals the fact of divine sovereignty in the exercise of election and reprobation, as already noted. And then we discover a strange and perplexing thing:

"As I live, says the Lord God, I have no pleasure in the death of the wicked, but that the wicked turn from his way and live; turn back, turn back, from your evil ways; for why will you die, O house of Israel?" (Ezek. 33:11). Can this be the same God whose predestination is revealed as governing election and reprobation?

Hear further: *"God our Savior desires all men to be saved and to come to the knowledge of the truth"* (I Tim. 2:4). *"Not wishing that any should perish, but that all should reach repentance"* (II Pet. 3:4).

"Come to me, all who labor and are heavy laden" Jesus urges, *"and I will give you rest. Take my yoke upon you, and learn of me; for I am gentle and lowly in heart, and you will find rest for your souls. For my yoke is easy, and my burden is light"* (Mat. 11:29-30). A genuine invitation? Of course! Made by God Himself!

Now we are in a riddle: 1) God does indeed hold us responsible for behavior in a universe under His absolute control. 2) He does determine who will, and who will not, obey His will. And yet, 3) He reveals His wish that all turn to Him and be saved. For our logic, the whole rational system bursts at the seams. Yet in the believer's experience, perfect harmony and great peace: **GOD RULES! BE NOT AFRAID!**

And Moses offers us something like an explanation: *"The secret things belong to the Lord our God; but the things that are revealed belong to us and to our children for ever, that we do all the words of this law"* (Deut. 29:29).

Note that what God reveals has but one purpose: we are called to *"do all the words of this law."* Our recognition of divine sovereignty is strong incentive to just that! God knows that we can find in revelation of His sovereignty the light, and power and inspiration requisite to the life of obedience. It steels the will to know that God is sovereign. It fortifies the emotions to know that He is forever at the helm of things, ever ruling, ever guiding, never outdone by the Evil One. It nurtures determination, especially in the face of opposition, to know that God has elected you to represent Him by way of good works in your time and place. It steels resolution to know that God does judge, both here and hereafter, and therefore no act is indifferent. Trust the Word. Bypass the idol intellect. Scoff at the doubts. And know that the "almighty" is also your "Father." What else matters?

The Father is also "Maker of heaven and earth"! Better look around. He made it all!

Does the Bible tell us how? Or is "science" our authority?

The Bible reveals that God created <u>by speaking</u>! But God did not say, "Bang!" That's "scientific" mythology.

Genesis tells us: *"And God said, 'Let there be light;' and there was light"* (Gen. 1:3). Note the method: *"And God said!"* He "said" what He wanted, and it was so. Not "Bang" and then a few billion years to arrive at the result: *"...for in six days the Lord made heaven and earth, the sea, and all that is in them"* (Ex. 20:11).

God speaks. Creation is! Turn to Genesis and read for yourself in chapter 1 how the pattern unfolds for the heavens, for the earth, for vegetation, for sun and moon and stars, for living creatures, and, in greater detail, for the making of man. God speaks; it is so!

Divine Speech is both instrument of all creation and on-going foundation of its being: *"By the word of the Lord the heavens were made, and all their host by the breath of his mouth"* (Ps. 33:6). *"Lift up your eyes on high,"* the Prophet commands, *"and see: who created these? He who brings out their host by number, calling them all by name; by the greatness of his might, and because he is strong in power not one is missing".* (Is. 40:26). *"...upholding the universe by his word of power"* (Heb. 1:3).

Speech is God's chosen means in creation and providence. And the Son of God, incarnate as Jesus Christ, is the "Word" through whom the divine Speech achieves its ends: *"In the beginning was the Word, and the Word was with God, and the Word was God. He was in the beginning with God; all things were made through him, and without him was not anything made that was made"* (John 1:1-2).

"And the Word became flesh and dwelt among us, full of grace and truth; and we beheld his glory, glory as of the only Son of the Father" (John 1:14).

When we are told in Genesis that God's method of creation was *"And God said...,"* and when we are told that the Word which is the vehicle of speech became our Lord and Savior Jesus Christ, it is the part of great wisdom not to run with the "Big Bang" crowd on the broad way. The more so when the Bible clearly tells us that the Word of spoken creation and the Word come in our flesh are one and the same: *"...in these last days he [God] has spoken to us by a Son, whom he appointed heir of all things, through whom also he created the world"* (Heb. 1:2). Can we choose the Word as Savior while declining to believe Him to be instrument of creation?

We must take time to reflect on the role which revelation assigns to "Word." We have thought about it before. But it would be hard to overstress the Bible's concentration upon what "Word" does.

Creation comes into being by the Word spoken. Word and "God said" are correlative.

"And God said...." That's not ancient history, nor primitive myth. From the beginning, Word was, and Word remains, at the heart and center of everything. Without words, the self would be nothing; without words, society would be impossible. Language, gift of God, is the fabric of life. Our words incarnate ideas just as God's Word created things.

Moreover, it is through Jesus Christ, the incarnate Word of God, that our salvation occurs. The Creed tells how. And it is through the Bible as inspired Word of God that we learn about it. Still more, by that Word the Holy Spirit makes believers fruitful in God's Kingdom.

It is not surprising, then, that the Creed comes in words. From "the beginning," Word is the pivot of life: *"In him [Jesus as Word] was life, and the life was the light of men"* (John 1:4). We find life in God's Word, we see by that Word, and when words are turned by the Devil into lies, those who are misled die by them. That is why Jesus calls the Devil, whose lie seduced Adam and Eve into sin, *"...a murderer from the beginning"* (John 8:44). That's the way it is. Choice is ever between the true Word and the lying word, and that is between "life," and "death." Also here.

God's Word tells us how He created heaven and earth: *"And God said...."* That's how creation was made and is sustained. Don't let the "murderer from the beginning" destroy you with words used as the lie, meant to deceive and destroy.

"And God said..." starts, and continues, it all. Remove words from our experience, and we say nothing, think nothing, are nothing. Remove God's Word from our experience, and we lose our way in the shadows of the world, and forfeit all hope of salvation. It's one Word: at creation, in the Incarnation, through the atonement and resurrection, as means of inspired revelation, as Light and Power unto the obedient and blessed life. By Word we are made and preserved, by word we learn, see and obey, by word we confess and we pray, by word we reveal who we are and whom we serve.

"And God said...." has from "the beginning" been foundation of all that is. Don't exchange that for some "scientific" piffle designed to rob you of the Power of His Word.

Our confession of God as "the Father almighty, maker of heaven and earth" sets us under certain obligations. Some are implied by our confession of this Article of the Creed, like these in the words of John Calvin:

> "We are not our own: let not our reason nor our will, therefore, sway our plans and deeds.
> "We are not our own: let us therefore not set it as our goal to seek what is expedient for us according to the flesh.
> "We are not our own: in so far as we can, let us therefore forget ourselves and all that is ours.
>
> "Conversely, we are God's: let us therefore live for him and die for him.
> "We are God's: let his wisdom and will therefore rule all our actions.
> "We are God's: let all the parts of our life accordingly strive toward him as our only lawful goal."

(<u>Institutes</u> III.7.1)

In addition:

We acknowledge that because every human being is God's possession, we are accountable to God for treating our own selves and others accordingly. His rules, not our ethical theories, prevail. This is the foundation of sound personal and social ethics, and operates through the conscience which is the Law of God inscribed, Calvin says, "on the fleshy tablets of the heart."

We acknowledge that, instead of clamoring for "rights"--a clamor which is now shredding society--we are born first of all with obligations, and understand that legitimate rights root only in duties required by God. The sequence is crucial: only <u>after</u> we assume the duties laid upon us by our creation may we speak of "rights." We are entitled to "rights" only to the degree that they are requisite to obedience to God.

We acknowledge whose is the world we inhabit. From the beginning man is called by the Creator to *"subdue"* the world for his own use (Gen. 1:28). *"Subdue"* surely implies prudent exploitation. God gives us the world for use. Those peoples who can make best use of it justify their claims to possession of the countries they inhabit. This rules out a sentimental disposition to romanticize the primitive. Small is not necessarily "beautiful." Preservation is not the name of the game. Expediently disciplined use is what the universe is for. While ab-use of the Creator's world is, of course, sin against the Creator, yet a judicious exploitation, based upon the *"subdue"* of the Creator, is the foundation of all creative, rather than restrictive, environmentalism.

And let us say that this Article of the Creed implies our being debtors in ways which ought to govern our behavior; we are:

1) <u>Cosmic debtors</u>: because we are born into a universe immense in size, infinite in variety, overwhelming in beauty, of endless potential situated by God in time and space. None of all this by our own making.

2) <u>Planetary debtors</u>: because we are born upon an earth aptly fitted to sustain and develop human life and to reward human work with abundance, uniquely provided for supplying the foundations for civilization and culture. None of this our own making.

3) <u>Social debtors</u>: because we are born into human society, affording a range from the rudiments of culture to the most sophisticated civilization, entering upon goods, sciences and arts, language and opportunities we have not created.

4) <u>Personal debtors</u>: because we are born into life, with intellect, will, the emotions, time and opportunity to put all to work, with eternal life the ultimate reward. None provided by ourselves.

5) <u>Spiritual debtors</u>: because we are born in the Image of the God who provides all of the above, and far more than we can realize, who makes provision for the restoration of fallen and debt-ridden man in the light focused upon us by the Creed. None our creation.

The recognition of debts such as these sends us to the Bible to find God's prescription for meeting our interest payments upon them. What do we owe Him, and His creation, mankind included?

To repeat: all demand for "rights" apart from recognition of the debts under which we are born and live is mindless chatter, egos blowing off steam. Rebellions are mounted upon such chatter, violence is brewed, death and destruction are afoot. But all the chaos and suffering which result from misplaced demand for "rights" only certify that genuine right arises out of commitment to genuine duty born of the debts listed above.

That is a message our times, like all times, need much to hear, and often repeated. Do your part in helping that along.

One of the secular tactics for getting the Bible off its back is the theory of biological evolution. It was designed to deal Genesis a death blow, and with it trust in the Scriptures. Darwin saw it that way, and so did Karl Marx who rejoiced on publication of Darwin's Origin Of Species in 1859. "This is the book that contains the natural-history foundation for our viewpoint," he writes to colleague Engels (Padover, Letters of Karl Marx, p. 139). And his viewpoint is avowedly atheistic!

So then, does the "I believe" in God as "Maker of heaven and earth" set us at odds with prevailing evolutionary theory?

Absolutely! How could it be otherwise?

Evolutionary theory imagines a universe begun with a Big Bang and a mankind arisen from some original slime along the route of animal ancestry. A fairy tale for adults, someone has said.

The Bible, to the contrary, reveals a Word-creation of all things and of man as specially molded out of the dust by God, inbreathed with life and gifted with His Image, with woman specially devised out of man's rib.

Pause now, step back, and think carefully: can the Genesis account of God's speaking the creation into existence be harmonized with a theory which imagines all things arising out of one explosion of energy along lines far from clear?

If both accounts were man's, perhaps some twisting of both could provide some kind of union. The effort is commonly called theistic evolution. But the Genesis account is not man's, but God's. To ignore or deny this is to surrender belief in the authenticity of God's Word. A Bible out of which you pick and choose only what you will believe is, of course, no authority at all.

Evolutionary theorizing postulates a God who is starkly at odds with His own Word. The Genesis revelation and the evolutionary hypotheses tread very different paths.

This faces the believer with a quite simple option. One we have faced before: God's Word, or man's? For the "I believe" that is an obvious choice. When you make it, you may learn how God's Word generates opposition and scorn.

Evolutionary theory has an absorbing attraction for minds bent on holiday from obligation to the demands of discipleship. With inflationary time at its disposal, evolutionary theory has expanded the "years" it assigns to theoretical developments from millions to billions with no end in view. The bank of time has unlimited resources for speculation, and no overdraft limits.

It's the usual: whose word? God's or man's?

Could God be, in fact, as we have confessed, a truly loving Father, and lie to us in Genesis as to how the world and all in it were made? He was there. We confess Him the Creator. If He preferred the evolutionary process, why should He not say so? Why say just the opposite? Why should the inspired Word of God begin with the Lie? That is the Devil's, not the Father's, stock in trade. What is there for a Father to hide?

Are you thinking, as is so often said, that of course the Bible is primitive myth and the writers knew no better? If so, the Bible has no authority at all, and Christianity itself is cast adrift. But then the Creed is without foundation and your "I believe" is indeed clutching at straws. But, as we have already considered, our "I believe" opens upon the only absolute certainty we can have because the Bible is in fact inspired by God the Holy Spirit, no myth at all, and as current and up-to-the-moment as your watch.

Yes, evolutionary theory has to dismiss the Bible. That is one reason it is so popular. But don't buy the argument that the Bible is a primitive collection of myths and memories. It is the most coherent, most sophisticated, most perceptive and authoritative source of Truth that the world has been given.

As we have already noted, God does not reveal Himself as saying, "Bang!" Evolutionists pin that on Him. He reveals Himself as having spoken all things into being through the Son, the Word who became our flesh and Savior. Through this Word God spoke, and upholds, all creation. Through this Word God provides for our re-creation as recounted by the Creed. Stay with the Word; don't run with the mob. The idol intellect has a special compulsion to demean the Bible and becloud revelation through the Word. For what Genesis reveals about the fallen state of man brands the intellect as fallible in ways it cannot endure nor, as fallen, correct. The Bible unclothes, as the old fable has it, intellect masquerading as king. Speculation is all show, full of sound and fury, signifying nothing.

The response is hatred. Down with the Bible! Out of our way! The popular weapon at the moment is the theory of evolution, endorsed everywhere by intellectuals themselves rebel servants of the intellect, furiously opposed to control by the Word of God.

Let them fulminate. Just quietly stand-under Genesis, and you will under-stand how the worlds, and you too, were made.

We must pause to reflect briefly upon the argument that "science" registers so much "success," that to prefer Genesis to evolutionary "science" is a venture in madness.

Is that so? Do the achievements of "science" spill over into validating the theory of evolution? Does sending men to the moon "prove" Darwin's hypothesis true?

Why should that be the case?

Indeed, true science serves mankind well, very well, in countless very practical applications. But that is in the form of "applied science." And have you ever noticed that applied science is always an exercise in <u>obedience</u> to divine law? It's not publicized much; but so it is.

Consider thoughtfully: if you wanted to build a bird coop, but cut the pieces in all different sizes could you put a coop together? No. Why not?

It's just a "law" which God instilled into His creation that measurements must match if the pieces are to combine into a usable coop. And so, in order to make your bird coop, you have to bow before God's natural law. Cut the pieces to fit, or you get no coop. That's the way it is with making things, and that's the way it is for all <u>applied</u> science. Obey the law, or it won't work!

"It's easy to make a philosophy;" said General Motors technical genius Charles Kettering, "it doesn't have to run." That applies equally to Darwinism and all the "scientific" speculation that so catches the public fancy. No one proves it, and no one can. But if true science is going to solve genuine problems, God's natural laws must be scrupulously discovered and obeyed. The applied sciences offer no proof that speculation like Darwinism is "scientific." Don't be taken in by claims that "science" proves this or that. Wait for it to "run."

Science serves human ends only to the degree that the scientist is obedient to the laws which God establishes for His universe. When obeyed, progress is the result. When disobeyed, chaos and disaster follow. Technological success says nothing about the accuracy of Darwinian and other hypotheses which are called "scientific" but are in fact nebulous theorizing, whistling in the dark corners of the universe, the Light of God's Word denied.

"God does not play dice with the universe," Einstein said in response to Heisenberg's "principle of indeterminacy." Indeed, if mankind were as obedient to God's Word incarnate in Scripture as applied science is to God's Word as incarnate in nature, how great progress would be.

INTERIM

STAGE,

AND CAST,

FOR HISTORY

What the Creed is now going to place upon our lips regarding Jesus Christ implies not only the creation, already confessed, but very specifically the Fall of man and its awesome consequences. It's all implicit in the Creed, but we can catch the "drift" more readily if we pause here briefly to sketch the great drama of human history begun with God's creation.

No TV sit-com, no play or opera or epic or novel, even from a most imaginative hand, in any way approaches in dramatic quality the background in history of what goes on within and about ourselves every hour. The shape given the present by mankind's early history governs how the eternal always touches us through the temporal, the unseen through the seen: *"The things that are seen are transient, but the things that are unseen are eternal"* (II Cor. 4:18).

As already observed, eternal destinies, our own included, are being shaped by us all, here and now, everywhere, in every moment of decision and act. Writing our eternal destiny in our every deed inscribed on the pages of passing time is, indeed, what time is for, and living is about. History is drama! Not only history in general, but ours in particular, the incalculable future hanging on decision to obey, or ignore, God's will. One of the clever devices of the Devil is to lull us into complete forgetfulness of all that. The idea of "pastime," says Catholic Father Ernest Dimnet, is sacrilegious. How little we know it. But the Devil does.

The Genesis revelation outlines the origins of the cosmic drama now going on all about us, and in which we all play our parts. It all began in the Garden of Eden. It all goes on to the Last Day. We will meditate upon the story in a series of "acts."

Act One. Making The Stage

God set the stage for history in His six-day Word-creation of the heavens and the earth. We have noted that. God spoke and it was so. His Speech is now vividly incarnate in a world thus called from nothing to being, a universe with warp and woof of natural law, and one suffused with energy and ablaze with light. In it, as the believer sees, God is everywhere.

Then God made the first two of all the human actors in history's drama, Adam and Eve, first parents of the human family: *"Then God said, 'Let us make man in our image, after our likeness"* (Gen. 1:26). Adam He made from the dust, breathing into his nostrils the breath of life.

Eve He made from Adam's rib (Gen. 2:21-22). Note that thus God carefully separated the human family from all other animal species. God would commit His own Son into the flesh thus distinguished from all other flesh. So Paul says to the Athenians: *"God has made of one blood all nations of men to dwell on all the face of the earth..."* (Acts 17:26). This He began by making Eve one with the blood of Adam, a blood that the Son will share by coming in human flesh.

Man and woman were made in God's Image. The implications are inexhaustible, but at least we know that thus the first pair were capable of communion with Him through language. The Word-using God makes His Image-bearers word-using creatures. Time He gave them, and talent for realizing their thoughts in the stuff of His world. God assigned them the task of *"subduing"* the creation (Gen. 1:28). And He placed them in a Garden called Eden, an earthly paradise. All was *"very good"* (Gen. 1:31).

Act Three. The Plot

God established the dramatic tension through a prohibition, a command for obedience laid upon our first parents.

Why He framed the plot as He did is not revealed. But we are told what the dramatic tension was, and this we may infer: God loved man and desired man's freely given love in return. Love of God bears the fruit of obedience to His will. *"If anyone loves me,"* Jesus says, *"he will keep my word..."* (John 14:11). Did Adam and Eve "love" their Creator? God gave them an easy opportunity to show Him by one very simple and specific act. So simple it was that the first couple had merely to restrain the impulse to act. Do nothing.

The dramatic tension revolved about what was later to become the First Commandment: *"You shall have no other gods before me."* (Ex. 20:3) Not for God's benefit, but for ours.

It became a choice just like those always facing ourselves: whose word will we heed?

There was, first of all, God's Word: *"The Lord God took the man and put him in the Garden of Eden to till it and keep it. And the Lord God commanded of the man, saying, 'You may freely eat of every tree in the garden; but of the tree of the knowledge of good and evil you shall not eat, for in the day that you eat of it you shall die'"* (Gen. 2:15-17).

A wholly unexpected dimension now appears. Another word is heard in the Garden. An Adversary to God appears. He takes the form of a serpent, and speaks through it! He is later called Satan and Devil (Rev. 12:9), and the Bible is notably reticent about his origins. Jude speaks of *"the angels that did not keep their own position but left their proper dwelling..."* (Jude 6). And Isaiah speaks of the *"Day Star, son of Dawn"* (Is. 14:12). But from whence he came we are not told.

"Now the serpent was more subtle than any other wild creature that the Lord God had made. He said to the woman (the story is told from Gen. 3:1 through 3:7), *"Did God say, 'You shall not eat of any tree in the garden?'"*.

That becomes, as already noted, the standard form of temptation across the centuries, in every situation: *"Did God say?"* Applied to the Bible it becomes: does He say through His Word?

The woman, not yet fallen, freely acknowledged that it was so:

"And the woman said to the serpent, 'We may eat of the fruit of the trees of the garden; but God said, "You shall not eat of the fruit of the tree which is in the midst of the garden, neither shall you touch it, lest you die."'"

The Devil was, as he always is, up to the opportunity, ready with the Lie which, Jesus says, makes him *"a murderer from the beginning"* (John 8:44)--for life or death is always at issue, in choice of Word or Lie.

Act Five. Temptation

"But the serpent said to the woman,'You will not die. For God knows that when you eat of it your eyes will be opened, and you will be like God, knowing good and evil'" (Gen. 3:1-5).

All the rest of the drama of history turns on the event now before us: Eve is tempted to disobey the Word of her Creator, and so is Adam. And disobey they do, to "Fall" out of that favor with God known as "life."

The Bible contrasts the consequences of choosing whose "word" to obey as choosing between "life" and "death." Obedience to God's Word through believing it is communion with God, the source of life. Disobedience to His Word is rejecting communion with God, which is death. Moses echoes for us this aboriginal choice: *"...therefore choose life...loving the Lord your God, obeying his voice..."* (Deut. 30:29-30).

63

"So when the woman saw that the tree was good for food, and that it was a delight to the eyes, and the tree was to be desired to make one wise, she took of its fruit and ate; and she also gave some to her husband, and he ate. Then the eyes of both were opened, and they knew that they were naked; and they sewed fig leaves together and made themselves aprons" (Gen. 3:6-7).

Notably, the serpent engages the woman, rather than the man, in conversation. St. Augustine, Calvin and others of the great theologians take note that the Fall followed upon Eve's taking authority upon herself in the first human family, though Adam had been made its head and she his *"help meet"* (Gen. 2:18). Her sin was compounded by Adam's following her lead. God says to him, *"Because you have listened to the voice of your wife, and have eaten of the tree of which I commanded you, 'You shall not eat of it,' cursed is the ground because of you'"* (Gen. 3:17).

The distinction which God makes is instructive. Eve's rebellion foretells radical feminism. Eve sins by usurping an authority not her own. Adam sins by letting go of the status of headship in which he was created.

Act Seven. Aftermath

So simply. So quietly. Man fell. Death entered history. Communion with God's enemy became the enduring competition for communion with God. Thus it is for every descendant of Adam and Eve to the end of time.

Suddenly realizing their nakedness, and now become aware of the sense of shame, the man and woman went in search for cover, sewing themselves *"breeches"* as a famous translation has it (the Geneva Bible) out of fig leaves (Gen. 3:7).

Their frantic search for protection foreshadowed how on the Last Day those who also thought themselves great enough to defy God will cry *"to the mountains and the rocks, 'Fall on us and hide us from the face of him who is seated on the throne, and from the wrath of the Lamb'"* (Rev. 6:16). Those who reject God have nothing but the inadequate stuff of creation to hide themselves, whether that be fig leaves or "science."

The Fall obliges God to publish through His Word His standards for male/female relations in society, beginning in Genesis and culminating in St. Paul: *"For the husband is the head of the wife as Christ is the head of the Church, his body, and is himself its Savior"* (Eph. 5:23). Eve ignored that in the Garden. So did Adam.

Radical feminism is not, obviously, a modern ideology. It began in the garden of Eden. Like Eve, rebels clothed in women's flesh resist divine order even though the woman's role as heart of the home offers her the most influential status among mankind. God has set the family at the center of society and made nurturing of youth key to social progress, with the mother at the center in the home.

The feminism which degrades home-building as "kitchen slavery" does the work of God's Adversary in dismantling the sinews which hold society together. Such feminism echoes the verdict of Eve's behavior, "Not God's will, but mine, be done!" The male's role as head of the home, and cutting edge in society, provides room for the female's investing social behavior with civility. As goes the home, so goes society. Motherhood, the key role of all, is to be nourished by loving fatherhood. That is Christian teaching on the home as central institution of civilization. Here the Image-bearers of God are nurtured. Could anything be more significant?

In her remarkable account of survival in the age of Stalin, entitled Hope Abandoned, Nadezhda Mandelstam, widow of murdered poet Osip Mandelstam, writes: "When the hard times came, it was suddenly clear how important women had been in ordering a man's daily life. Whatever fancy airs they may have given themselves, they were the builders and mainstay of the home. In this there was no difference between a rich woman and the humblest peasant's wife" (p. 105).

The biblical confrontation with radical feminism is unmistakable, and earns Genesis and Paul and the Bible in general bitter feminist scorn, neatly bolstered by the theory of evolution and higher biblical criticism. The believer has to live with that. The choice between the radical feminist conception of woman's role in the family and the biblical conception is just another "either/or" of Christianity. Make the choice, and stand by it. Loss of the centrality of the family, as it now occurs in the Western world, if unchecked, foredooms our society to the totalitarian state, of which God has given us foretaste in Stalin, Hitler and such.

Recall that when Moses' sister Miriam leads his brother Aaron in rebellion against Moses, it is she who is struck with leprosy: *"And they said, 'Has the Lord indeed spoken only through Moses? Has he not spoken through us also?'"* (Num. 12:2). Aaron indeed held "office" in Israel, not Miriam: *"Behold, Miriam was leprous, as white as snow"* (v. 10). Moses intercedes, Aaron confesses sin, and Miriam is finally restored. God rejects radical feminism.

And so St. Paul: *"I permit no woman to teach or have authority over men; she is to keep silent. For Adam was formed first, then Eve; and Adam was not deceived, but the woman was deceived and became a transgressor"* (I Tim. 2:12-14).

What could have been so wrong, from human perspective, with sampling delicious fruit--with the breeze cool, the sky blue, and birds singing? Just as what could be wrong with harmless speculation on human origins, or with women wanting to be other than they were meant to be?

One thing wrong, really, not quite hidden by the beauty of Eden, not quite hidden by the appeal of rebellion: simply choosing to obey an authority other than God: Eve obeys the serpent; Adam knuckles under to Eve; radical feminism yields to its own instincts. Sin has only one trade-mark: the Word of God is flouted. The day you disobey, God said then and says now, you die! What happens thereafter is the behavior of the spiritually deceased, reckless in its devastation of social good.

We have noted that the Adam and Eve suddenly saw what they had not anticipated seeing--their own nakedness, implying their own fragility, their inability to make it on their own. They sensed their own guilt in defiance of their Creator. They were not like God at all. They had been taken in by the him whom Jesus, as we know, describes as *"a murderer from the beginning..."* because he is *"a liar and a father of lies"* (John 8:44). What puny, helpless creatures they saw themselves to be, out on their own. Just as puny as are the cynical, the skeptical, the foolishly learned, the arrogant who today mouth the same old, weary *"Did God say?"* against divine revelation and divine Law.

Cut off from the sustaining love of God by way of flouting His command, what had they left? Nothing between them and the God on whom they were totally dependent, and whom they had just rebuffed. They were naked indeed, with a nudity of body and spirit not at all compensated by the husks of the fig tree hastily made into *"aprons"* (Gen. 3:7).

So our first parents hid, hoping somehow to get by unseen. See how great a Fall! The Image-bearers of God, alive in His favor, become cowering creatures alien to their Maker. And God saw, called, passed judgment and expelled them from the Garden. Time and history begin. Our time and our history, too.

God's threat had been, *"In the day that you eat of it [the forbidden fruit] you shall die"* (Gen. 2:17).

Adam and Eve ate. Did Adam and Eve really die, then?

Yes, of course! God was not bluffing; He never is.

What St. Paul is inspired to call the "last enemy," death, was introduced into history by mankind's Fall. It remains man's last enemy until time itself passes away.

And we learn now something about the biblical conception of "death." Visibly in existence, bodily active, our parents were none-the-less alien from God, whom to "know" is life. Medieval artists pictured man's inherited state as the "Dance Of Death," men and women seemingly alive but in fact spiritually cut off from God, a living death.

"Death" is an alienation from God of which bodily demise is ultimate symbol. The tomb is lasting witness to man's Fall; the awesome silence of physical death mutely testifies to God's penalty upon disobedience. One hears nothing in cemeteries but the melancholy sighing of the wind. Is it whispering, *"Did God say...?"*

Indeed, Adam and Eve kept on moving about and talking, even with God. But their relation with Him was radically changed. At the forbidden tree their posture had been, 'Not Thy will, but ours, be done.' That was, and is, sin. Its fruit was, and is, alienation from God the source of life: *"The wages of sin is death"* (Rom. 6:23). Spiritually, Adam and Eve were dead, a heritage they passed on to all mankind. In due season, that separation from God was reflected also in their physical decease. Why the delay?

Because God had chosen to make that interim between physical birth and physical death a time of opportunity to hear the Word of Life. The Church has generally thought of Adam and Eve as having done so. We will call it God's sacramentalizing of His world. Paul can continue on after warning that *"The wages of sin is death,"* to say, *"but the free gift of God is eternal life in Christ Jesus our Lord"* (Rom. 6:21). It was for Adam and Eve also.

What emerges from the Fall is a universe devoted by its Maker into opportunity for restoration to lost life.

We are calling that the sacramental character of God's world.

It was not until another Man, in another Garden, said in anticipation of the Cross, *"...nevertheless, not my will, but thine, be done"* (Luke 22:42) that sin was confronted and atoned by the Lord Jesus' crucifixion, and the threat of spiritual death removed from those who by faith died on the Cross in Him.

However long time endures, all history is but epilogue to that fatal moment in the original Garden when man said No to God and Yes to the Devil. All that follows in the Creed revolves about that step from life into death, and how God undertakes to annul it with a step into life for those who believe.

God might have ended it all on that fatal day. He did choose to destroy, later, by way of the Flood, all mankind save Noah and his family, when He found human iniquity unendurable (Gen. 6:13).

But we may cautiously ask, suppose God had erased His creation at the Fall? Any other Image-bearer in any other world would be faced with the same choice: who has your love, that is whom would you serve? For God made man free for the very purpose of enabling us freely to choose Him as Master. It is, indeed, only in that free obedience to God which is love that the Image-bearer can become who we are meant to be: *"And you shall love the Lord your God with all your heart, and with all your soul, and with all your might"* (Deut. 6:5, quoted in Mat. 22:27, Mark 12:30, Luke 10:27).

God chose not to destroy His creation but rather to make His world sacramental. What is that?

God chose to keep the creation as the arena in which our final destiny is determined. How we put to use the world which God sustains for that purpose determines whom we love and serve--God or another. Thus all things become sacramental, that is our use of all things acquires an everlasting spiritual dimension. God sustains the universe to confront us with constant choice, that between obedience to His Word and rejection of that Word.

Two "cities" appear in human history, in the language of St. Augustine, the City of God and the City of Earth: "These two cities were made by two loves: the earthly city by the love of self unto contempt of God, and the heavenly city by the love of God unto the contempt of self" (Bk. 14, 28). Citizenship in the City of God sacramentalizes the creation; citizenship in the City of Earth confirms the penalty of death in disobedience.

Time and circumstance now put the question: how will you use God's world: in obedience or disobedience? Not for the sake of the world! That is passing away, even at this moment. But for determining the destiny of your own self. Each day poses the question, *"Did God say?"* And each day records your answer.

We must take careful note of the believer's sacramental relation to God's creation. Involved in that is the right perception of the "good works" which we are required to do.

It is an easy and common mistake to view "good works" in themselves. We tend to focus upon those who may benefit by them--say other people, say endangered species, even an endangered planet. But we thus forget that the beneficiaries of our good works do not endow our obedience with lasting value. Both the works and those who benefit from them are temporal, passing swiftly away.

God's command to do good does indeed benefit the needy, the oppressed, the habitat and environment. But the divine mandate does not thus exhaust its meaning. A good work finds its ultimate meaning in the doer, not the receiver. The work is temporal; the doer, eternal. The deed, whatever its nature, finds ultimate meaning in the effect which the doing, the obedience, has upon the self of the doer. In a sacramental world all that we do affects finally the destiny of our selves.

Christianity is not concerned to effect "earth-keeping" as such, or conservation or charitable performance. These find value only in obedience by the doer to God's will as revealed in His Word.

Social welfare, environmentalism, justice and charity are indeed fruits of Christianity, but only as by-products left behind the self enroute to eternity. The Church is not some form of the welfare state. It is teacher and guide to the life of obedience. And it is to make obedience possible that God sustains His world and all who live within it.

In obedience to the divine command to *"love your neighbor as yourself"* (Luke 10:27 and elsewhere), obedient believers do indeed good works to their neighbors. And society is thus beneficiary of Christian love, while the obedient doer thus invests in the coin of eternity. But the good work, with its recipient, passes away. What lasts is the self of the obedient doer. And what lasts, also, is the self of the selfish, unloving non-doer.

It is the universe as sacramental that discriminates obedience from disobedience with eternal consequences upon both.

The bridge between inherited death and available life is "I believe." The content of that bridge is unfolded in the Creed. Each article reveals yet another step taken by God to enable those who believe to make of our daily use of the universe a sacrament unto life eternal.

Dull and monotonous as our moments may seem, each one is always at a climax of the drama of life: in every act of thought, word, deed, at issue is this: whose script is being followed--God's or the Devil's, perhaps masquerading as our own? This is why Jesus warns us of the importance of even the seemingly insignificant: *"I tell you, on the day of judgment men will render account for every careless word they utter..."* (Mat. 12:36). There are no neutral moments.

How God chooses to achieve re-birth of His Image in those whose "I believe" opens them to His Word and Spirit is summed up in what now follows in the Creed, to the end that those who through believing strive to do His Word may receive *"the right to the tree of life"* (Rev. 22:14).

There are two sides to our confession of each article of the Creed. One side will be the gracious activity of God on our behalf; the other side will be what the necessity for such divine action reveals about who and what we are.

Let not our rejoicing in salvation blind us to how desperately we are in need of saving. The better we see that, the more genuine will be our thanksgiving and dedication to the life of obedience.

Article 2.

AND IN JESUS CHRIST,

HIS ONLY BEGOTTEN SON,

OUR LORD

Let us pause to consider carefully--for salvation hinges on it--the combination of titles which the Creed is going to choose for our confession of believing in the Second Person of the Holy Trinity. We will discuss each separately after briefly summarizing them here to exhibit the inner coherence among them.

1.   We first say, "Jesus." This name confesses Him as our Savior. He saves His people from their sins.

2.   We next say, "Christ." This, obviously, is not repetition for Savior. We step beyond Savior to Messiah, the anointed. We thus confess that He relates to us in three unique ways: a) He is our Prophet, or Teacher, on how to turn the gift of salvation into a life of discipleship; b) He is our Priest, or Advocate, forever at our side and before the Father on our behalf; and, c) King, who rules with absolute authority all things in heaven and upon earth.

3.   And then we add, "our Lord." We mean that He not only saves from sin, and for obedience, but that to Him all will one day bow the knee, to Him we yield the heart and tune the will, whose approval is our joy, whose service is our freedom, whose benediction is our blessing, and whose absolute right to govern our every act we freely acknowledge and strive to obey.

4.   Finally, we confess Him as the one who will come to "judge the living and the dead."

Some conclusions flow from this combination of divinely assigned titles:

1.   He is our "Jesus" only to be our "Christ." If He is not our Prophet, Priest and King in daily life, He is not our Savior for eternity.

2.   He is "Jesus" and "Christ" only for those who also serve Him as Lord, seeking out His will, confessing their delinquencies, repenting their sins, striving ever more to serve Him.

3.   Because in Him as Jesus liberation from the guilt of depravity and sin is possible, and because in Him as Christ all the resources for a new life of obedience are available, He will finally be our Judge as to what use we made of all He has done and does for us. It's a fair question, isn't it: "what have you done with all that I did for you?"

"Now the birth of Jesus Christ took place in this way," writes St. Matthew. "When his mother Mary had been betrothed to Joseph, before they came together she was found to be with child of the Holy Spirit; and her husband Joseph, being a just man and unwilling to put her to shame, resolved to divorce her quietly. But as he considered this, behold, an angel of the Lord appeared to him in a dream, saying, 'Joseph, son of David, do not fear to take Mary your wife, for that which is conceived in her is of the Holy Spirit; she will bear a son, and you shall call his name Jesus, for he will save his people from their sins.'" (Mat. 1:20-21).

It's the angel's definition: His name "Jesus" means <u>Savior</u>, *"for he will save his people from their sins."*

Therefore John the Baptist, forerunner of the Savior, can introduce Him to the world in the words, *"Behold, the Lamb of God, who takes away the sin of the world!"* (John 1:29). His reference is to the Jewish religious system in which a lamb is sacrificed to expiate sin, a prefiguring of Jesus' death on Calvary. *"Indeed, under the Law almost everything is purified with blood, and without the shedding of blood there is no forgiveness of sins"* (Heb. 9:22). This is because *"the blood is the life"* (Deut. 12:23), and death is the divine penalty upon sin, a penalty symbolized in the sacrifice of a lamb, and realized in the death of Jesus.

Of supreme interest to each of us is, did He die for me? And the answer is simply, YES, IF: 1) you believe so, meaning 2) that claim finds validation in your behavior as "new" selves, through acts governed by the Word of divine revelation employed for the purpose by the indwelling Spirit.

He was, indeed, the Father's *"Suffering Servant,"* so vividly portrayed in Isaiah 53, but, remember, not ours!

Don't fall into the easy and common mistake of trying to twist Jesus our "savior" into Jesus our "servant." It is easy enough to "accept" Him as free pass to eternal life. Raise a hand; come forward; fall on your knees--and it's all done! Salvation in your grasp. Jesus your willing slave, riding on His back into heaven! Shame!!

Yes, He does save His people from their sins. But who are "His people"? They are those who are "saved" to "serve," that is, as we have been saying, for lives of good works. Our Lord puts on our lips His own summary: *"Thy kingdom come, Thy will be done, on earth...."* For this we are "saved." In doing this is salvation. Detours around a life of obedient "good works" lead to hell. If a serious prayer, *"Thy will be done,"* then a serious commitment, "beginning with me." Saved to serve, or not saved at all.

Our salvation depends upon making no mistake about what our Lord came for and expects in return.

Let us be reminded of the model laid out in the Exodus of Israel from bondage in Egypt: 1) liberation by God through Moses as exemplar of Christ, followed by 2) instruction by God through Moses from Mount Sinai how the liberated life was to be lived in obedience to His will--the Ten Commandments (Ex. 20, Deut. 5). And, 3) with the whole Bible as God's Manual for applying the Law to the consecrated life which He expects from the believer freed in Jesus Christ. The biblical Manual reveals both the Savior and the new life which "being saved" implies.

Jesus Himself connects believing to obedience: *"Then Jesus said to the Jews who had believed in him, 'If you continue in my word, you are truly my disciples, and you will know the truth, and the truth will make you free'"* (John 8:31-32). Notice well: 1) they "believed" in Him; and 2) starting from there, He requires of them obedience to His Word. Believing is not the end but the beginning. And then, 3) obedience itself is the ultimate freedom, leading into life eternal.

We have noticed that Christianity always sets an either/or before us. Choose God's Word or another's.

Now we observe that Christianity also sets a both/and before us: both saved "from" burden and guilt, and saved "for" the life of priestly obedience in trying to govern each choice by His Word.

In countless ways, often very subtle and seemingly pious ways, "Jesus" is played off against His own Word as being, really, the way around the Bible. Watch for it, and beware!

To miss this "from...for" connection is to pervert what the Bible comes to reveal. Jesus does not command us to put Him on the throne of our hearts; He commands us to "continue in my word." Why? Because a Jesus enthroned by ourselves is always subject to our whims. The Bible, not the imagination, is key to "knowing" Jesus and having a so-called "personal" relationship with Him. *"If a man loves me,"* Jesus says, *"he will keep my word..."* (John 14:23). Always the Bible is the bridge which unites believer and Savior, and always obedience to the Word is the form in which that unity appears. The Bible which governs how we think, how we speak and act, is the sinew of personal union between you and the Lord. You need not imagine any other bond.

If "are you saved?" means anything, it implies, "are you striving every moment to live in conscious obedience to the Word of God?" As we have already heard: *"For we are his workmanship, created in Christ Jesus for good works, which God prepared beforehand that we should walk in them"* (Eph. 2:10). "Being saved" is doing those "good works" for which we have been "created in Christ Jesus." As Paul warns: *"Be not deceived; God is not mocked, for whatever anyone sows, that he will also reap"* (Gal. 6:7). And he says this in a letter which some people say relieves us of obedience to the Law!

Notice, too, that for the Bible "good works" are not as we might define them, but as God "prepared beforehand," that is as defined by His Law and Scriptures.

Notice, now, how the Creed does indeed mirror us to ourselves: to confess Jesus Christ as "Savior" acknowledges that we desperately need a Savior! It is confession that we cannot reach the end for which the human being is made by our own resources. We can neither define the "good," nor find the way to it, nor even strive to do it short of finding a "Savior" in Jesus Christ.

In theological terms, "saved" in Jesus Christ appears in two facets:

Saved "from," called justification, and saved "for," called sanctification.

Justification means being viewed by God as cleansed from the guilt of sin. Justification is liberation from the guilt of sin as inherited from the Fall, and as incurred by our own daily disobedience to God's revealed will. "Saved" in this sense implies confession of and repentance for sin and a "washing away" of the stains of disobedience, as symbolized by baptism. Justification implies the incomprehensible grace of being viewed by God, not as we are in ourselves, but in His Son to whom we are joined by the "I believe." In consequence, *"being justified by faith, we have peace with God through our Lord Jesus Christ"* (Rom. 5:1). Joy rises out of the gift of looking upon our own selves, through the grime of evils that still besmirch us, to find peace with God through the forgiveness of sins in Christ Jesus. And thus renewed to take up daily the duties of obedience.

The fact that justification comes by faith is easily misconstrued as ruling out good works. This, as already stressed, is a fatal mistake. Just because we are unable to provide for our own justification, it is supposed that we need not pursue obedience. All is paid for. A deadly error. One that accounts in large measure for the weakness of the Church in the world. The "good news" is that we are freed to get at *"Thy will be done on earth,"* not that we are en route to bliss. The Last Judgment will not be an inquiry, indeed, into whether justification was available. But rather how we used the liberation won in Jesus for us.

Justified we are, indeed, through faith, but Paul warns us, *"If I have all faith, so as to remove mountains, and have not love, I am nothing"* (I Cor. 13:2). And "love" means, as we know, obedience.

So we turn now to sanctification.

Justification opens the way to pursuit of life eternal through obedience to divine law, that is as we have already discussed, the life of good works. We will discover, indeed, that such pursuit is also beyond our power without the aid of the Holy Spirit, but the aspiration for it is possible through faith. God can therefore command our keeping His commandments, and Jesus can say that this is what loving Him means. But as we try to do that, we discover how desperately necessary is the power which only God can give, and does give via His Word by His Spirit.

We are "saved for," then, what the Church has long called sanctification, that is growing into true human-ness by "walking" in the Word of God through the indwelling power of the Holy Spirit. The "sanctified" person, that is the saint, is en route to being the truly human we were created to be. "Saints" there are in the world, not common but models. You know when you meet them.

It is a life-long journey. We learn what St. Paul means by saying, *"Not that I have already obtained this or am already perfect; but I press on to make it my own, because Christ Jesus has made me his own. Brethren, I do not consider that I have made it my own; but one thing I do, forgetting what lies behind and straining forward to what lies ahead, I press on toward the goal for the prize of the upward call in Christ Jesus. Let those of us who are mature be thus minded..."* (Phil. 3:12-15).

We can look upon the Creed as guide to the kind of maturity that the Apostle has in mind. And we can look upon our pursuit of the wisdom implicit in the Creed as obedience to his command to be "thus minded."

And we can take encouragement from a most surprising and unexpected thing. It is this: the great Apostle also had his struggles with the life of priestly self-denial. Take courage! And go on!

It is most remarkable!

Something you would never expect. At least, not at first. Later, perhaps, when you sense the flavor of sainthood, you can read Paul's account as in accord with your own experience.

Listen: *"I do not understand my own actions. For I do not do what I want, but I do the very thing I hate. Now if I do what I do not want, I agree that the law is good. So then it is no longer I that do it, but sin which dwells within me. For I know that nothing good dwells within me, that is, in my flesh. I can will what is right, but I cannot do it. For I do not do the good I want, but the evil I do not want is what I do. Now if I do what I do not want, it is no longer I that do it, but sin which dwells in me"* (Rom. 7:15-20).

There are those who foolishly insist that this description of himself could only befit the Saul of the pre-Damascus road, the Saul who had not yet met the risen Lord in the blinding light of revelation. The Dutch pastor Jacobus Arminius, whose mistaken teaching on the doctrine of divine predestination occasioned the great Synod of Dordt (1618-1619), denied that Romans 7 described the "converted" Paul. So have many others. How could it be the Paul who inscribed the great epistles, Romans included?

But then, of course, Paul's self-assessment loses all creative power for us. We will have no Damascus road. We will struggle on, finding Paul's description of himself all too true of ourselves, blind to his way out. Happily, Romans chapter 7 is one of the great inspirations along the way of the common Christian life. For the Apostle goes on thus: *"Wretched man that I am! Who will deliver me from this body of death? Thanks be to God through Jesus Christ our Lord! So then, I myself serve the law of God with my mind, but with my flesh I serve the law of sin"* (Rom. 7: 24).

How true it is! There is, in fact, for every believer a nagging contradiction between confession and performance. A gap yawns between 1) the words of the Creed to which we give brave assent and, 2) the governing of our behavior by those words and the Scriptures. We manage to live along, most of the time, without attending too closely to the contradiction between confession and behavior which troubled Paul so much. But we do get intimations of imperfection, and may even sense how "wretched" is our obedience. And, then, in such moments of beholding in the mirror of the Creed just how far short we come of the life of joy, peace and obedience, we remember that Paul felt the same way. And we see that he points us to the antidote, the antidote of the Creed: Jesus came as Savior! Jesus reigns as Savior!

O great joy! Twice repeated: Once, if Paul fails so miserably and goes on, then we! Twice, if for him, then for us, "Thanks be to God through Jesus Christ our Lord!" We, too, can be--and are--"delivered" from sin and failure. To help us see, and say so is the great message of the Creed.

Rejoice!

They are, so to speak, siblings: justification for the purpose of sanctification. Neither without the other; both the purpose of Jesus' coming and the spread of Christianity around the world.

And now we can foresee why (as the Creed will lead us to say) the Son comes not only as "Jesus" but also as "Christ." God's Son as the "Jesus" in whom we believe liberates us, by dying for us, from the burden and bondage of sin, that is disobedience to the divine will: justification! And God's Son as "Christ" guides us into the life of productive citizenship in the Kingdom of God: sanctification. For by ourselves, even as liberated, we do not know: what is such "citizenship"? How learned? How attained? For this we need, and are given, Jesus as the Christ.

The Creed moves us inexorably 1) through the "Jesus" who saves us "from" the guilt of sin, and "for" the life of obedience, 2) on to the "Christ" who governs that life of obedience, and 3) then on to the "Lord" who rules and 4) the Judge who comes to monitor our performance. All inseparable parts of one piece, the Christian life entered through the "I believe" of the Creed.

We may pause to reflect, especially as we attend to what so often passes for "evangelism," and pose the question: is all we have been thinking about really a correct reading of the Creed? Might it not be some misconstruction of the Gospel? Is not "Gospel" defined as the "Good News" of salvation? Is not salvation "free"? Why, then, talk of obedience and judgment? Are we not "saved" by faith alone, as Luther (mis)translates Romans 5:1?

No doubt the best response to such queries is to move on into the Creed and listen. We do say "Jesus," and then "Christ," and then "Lord," and at last "Judge."

Why?

The Creed is in fact a notably brief document. Why have us confess the Son in four forms, unless each form clearly pertains to our salvation?

God's Son comes not only as Jesus, meaning Savior, but as Christ, meaning the Anointed, the promised Messiah.

Why so? Isn't a Savior enough?

Indispensable, but not enough. If the "Jesus" were enough, then the "Christ" would not be in the Creed. Jesus came as Savior, we may be sure, only in order to be our Christ, meaning our Prophet-Priest-King. We need the second as much as the first. Along no other route than from "Jesus" to "Christ" is our salvation possible: *"I am the way, the truth and the life; no one comes to the Father, but by me"* (John 14:6).

The term "Christ" warns us against abuse of the Gospel. It is easy to welcome the "Gospel" interpreted as "good news." Good news makes no enemies, and the distribution of "freebies" draws crowds. Who doesn't warm to a "Savior," especially one who comes, as it were, free of charge, even perhaps begging to be accepted, His message crafted to what people are willing to hear? The "hawking" of Jesus on street corners like "cheap Jack's wares," said Dietrich Bonhoeffer, the German pastor-martyr, too readily passes for evangelism.

But, this seductive mistake is shattered by the term "Christ."

And, if in truth our "I believe in Jesus" does liberate us for His service, then we do welcome the "I believe in Christ" as defining what acceptable service is: *"And by this we may be sure that we know him, if we keep his commandments"* (I John 2:3). The Christ applies those "commandments" to the behavior of those "saved" by Jesus.

Our confession of "I believe" in Jesus as the <u>Christ</u> is an admission that even if freed from guilt and bondage to sin in Jesus, we cannot on our own find and follow the road to discipleship without faith in the Christ.

We are warned, for example, in the tenth chapter of First Corinthians, and in the third chapter of Hebrews, and again in Jude verse 5, that liberation is not enough. These passages all stress that most of those liberated by God out of Egypt--the model of the believer's liberation in Jesus--failed to enter upon the Promised Land! Think on it! Freed from Pharaoh, yet they died in the wilderness, which represents for us the kind of world in which we live. The potential of their liberation was never realized.

Why not? Were they not liberated from Pharaoh? Yes! Were they not gone out of Egypt, the house of bondage? Yes! What went wrong then? Just this: Israel did not real-ize its liberation from bondage in the freedom of obedience.

Paul goes so far as to say that those who came out of Egypt enjoyed the sacrament of baptism by passing through the Red Sea, and the sacrament of the Lord's supper in eating the heavenly Manna and drinking from the water miraculously flowing from the Rock in the wilderness *"which Rock was Christ"* (I Cor. 10:4, with ref. to Ex. 17:6, Num. 20:11). And yet, the Apostle says: *"With many of them God was not well pleased, for they were overthrown in the wilderness. Now, these things are warnings for us, not to desire evil as they did"* (I Cor. 10:1-6). That is, not to abuse our freedom for self-indulgence.

We need the Christ as Prophet (that is Teacher), as Priest (that is Advocate with the Father) and as King (that is ruling our every choice) if we are *"to make our calling and election sure"* (II Pet. 1:10).

Let us carefully contemplate what this means.

By confession of the "Christ," we confess that justification in Jesus is not the end but the beginning. Just as Israel found that liberation from Egypt was not the culmination of God's work for them but the beginning of opportunity to serve Him. Just as He had said to Pharaoh via Moses: "Let my people go...."

Why?

"That they may serve me in the wilderness" (Ex. 7:16).

That is why He liberates us, too, from bondage to world, flesh and Devil: to serve Him in the wilderness of this world. The Christ tells us how.

The Church has long spoken of the three "offices," that is functions on our behalf, of Christ in the life of the believer. We have already briefly mentioned them:

1. The Christ as <u>Prophet</u>: that is, as Teacher, via the Scriptures, of all that we must know about our creation, Fall, depravity, redemption in Him and life of obedience to Him, none of which could we find out by ourselves. The "I believe in Christ" is a confession of ignorance, and of openness to the Truth revealed to remedy it. What ignorance, for example? Say a secular ignorance of my origin, my depravity, my trespass upon God's time and world; and my ignorance of God's remedy for sinfulness, how it is to be received, and what response to salvation God requires. In short, what is summarized by the Creed. None of this can I know save through receiving the Word of Christ as Prophet, whose illumining Scripture comes under the direction of the Spirit to control my thought. Nor is this an abstract information about mankind in general; it is precise prescription for who I am, how I am to be saved, and how, as saved, I am to live. And exactly the same for you.

And we must not make the mistake of thinking that the living Christ will illumine and direct us through no effort of our own, as Luther sometimes advises: if the Bible is a closed book for us, then the Christ is no Prophet of ours. Let us not delude ourselves. Nor must we be misled by "prophets" who claim special revelations in the "God said to me..." fashion. Believe them not!

Through the Son as Word, God speaks out of the Scriptures to those who accept them by faith. Christ as Prophet, then, implies the whole scope of the Bible. It is this Jesus has in mind in commissioning His Church to "teach" disciples *"all that I have [as Christ] commanded you"* (Mat. 28:20).

The Christ is also Priest on our behalf.

As "Jesus," that is "Savior," He "takes away the sins of the world." He is the Highpriest who sacrifices Himself on the altar of Calvary, fulfilling the pre-vision of the Jewish sacrificial system.

After His ascension to heaven, Jesus serves His people as Priest in another manner. The biblical Israelite priest: a) represented others to God, and offered sacrifices for their sin. So the Christ, at the right hand of the Father, appeals to His personal sacrifice as Jesus to clothe all believers in His spotless garment; and, b) a priest serves as on-going mediator between God and man, a living bridge across the gulf which our daily waywardness opens and re-opens between God and ourselves. So Jesus the Christ now serves in heaven, ever alert to our slips and falls to appease them in Himself before the Father. But, of course, we suffer such slips and falls, and therefore need the Christ as Priest, only if we indeed are seeking, every hour, to know and do the divine will. Else the confession "I believe in Christ" is meaningless.

We already observe how much of the meaning of "Jesus Christ" is left out if concentration is fixed only upon "Jesus" as Savior, that is, really, as our Servant. And we see clearly enough why the Creed does not stop with belief in "Jesus."

Indeed, the Creed is making clear that the Son of God is "Jesus" Savior only for those who also find in Him the "Christ" who is Prophet and Priest and, next, King.

We need, also, the Christ as King: *"Why do you call me, 'Lord, Lord,'" Jesus exclaims in exasperation, "and do not do what I tell you?"* (Luke 6:46).

Here He speaks not only as Savior, not only as Teacher, not only as Priest to heal our failures, but also as King whose Word is to be obeyed by those who claim to believe in Him.

Here, as they say, the cards are on the table. Why celebrate Jesus as Savior if we ignore the Christ as King? What avails it for us gladly to "accept" Jesus unless at the same time we become eager to be governed by Him? He is plain about it: *"If you love me, you will keep my commandments"* (John 14:15). The quality of our gratitude for justification in Jesus is reflected and measured by the reality of our will to obey Christ unto sanctification. The Kingship of Christ invests His inspired Word with absolute and awesome authority.

The role of a king is to rule. As glorious as is His role as Savior, so awesome is His office as King. St.John records in Revelation the vision of the risen Christ given him on the Isle of Patmos: *"He is clad in a robe dipped in blood, and the name by which he is called is the Word of God.... From his mouth issues a sharp sword with which to smite the nations, and he will rule them with a rod of iron; he will tread the wine press of the fury of the wrath of God the Almighty. On his robe and on his thigh he has a name inscribed, King of kings and Lord of lords"* (Rev. 19:13,15-16).

To this fearsome King, we learn from Paul, on the day of final judgment, *"Every knee will bow...and every tongue confess that Jesus Christ is Lord..."* (Phil. 2:10-11). *"...and thus let us offer to God acceptable worship, with reverence and awe; for our God is a consuming fire"* (Heb. 12:28-29).

To worship is simply to obey. Acceptable worship is obedience done under the aegis of the revealed Word.

We see that the Creed has moved us far beyond the emotional binge of "accepting" Jesus, to a confrontation with what that implies when perceived as bringing us under the dominion of "Christ."

"In this was manifested the love of God toward us," writes St. John, "that God sent his only begotten Son into the world, that we might live through him. Herein is love, not that we loved God, but that he loved us, and sent his Son to be the propitiation for our sins" (I John 4:9-10).

Why mention <u>only begotten</u>?

It is, first of all, to stress the uniqueness of Jesus Christ. And, second, to warn the believer against all other "saviors" of mankind. There is only one Jesus Christ. Only one who can say, *"I am the way, the truth, and the life; no one comes to the Father but through me"* (John 14:6).

Yes, the Bible knows others who are called *"sons"* of God, like Adam (Luke 3:38), like the children of Israel who are called by God *"my first-born son"* (Ex. 4:22), like the mysterious *"sons of God [who] shouted for joy"* at the creation (Job 38:7), as indeed like believers themselves who are called *"sons of God"* (I John 3:1).

The only begotten Son, Jesus Christ, *"is not ashamed to call them brethren"* (Heb. 2:11) who believe in Him. Yet, He is not just one among this large family, though they be *"joint heirs"* with Himself (Rom. 8:17). He is uniquely, and solely, Son of God. He is uniquely, and solely, "begotten" of God who promises Him, *"Ask of me, and I will make the nations your heritage, and the ends of the earth your possession. You shall break them with a rod of iron, and dash them in pieces like a potter's vessel"* (Ps. 2:7-9).

Let the feeling sink in that Jesus Christ, and God His Father, and Christianity itself is far from being all gush and mush. God is, to the unbelieving, a *"consuming fire."* And Jesus the Christ as Lord is quite capable of dashing His enemies *"in pieces like a potter's vessel."*

Christianity, like life itself, is serious business.

We can fool ourselves, and perhaps fool others, about taking the life of obedience seriously. But God is not mocked.

Remember it.

The only begotten Son alone can say, *"I am the way, and the truth, and the life; no one comes to the Father, but by me"* (John 14:6).

Why does the Creed add this phrase to the already penetrating impact of "Jesus Christ"?

Because the Creed intends to make here, as it were, an excursion for sake of emphasis. It is to stress that both as Jesus and as Christ, the Son of God is <u>Lord</u>. Perhaps it dots the i, as they say, or crosses the t, summing up together what is taught us in the names Jesus and Christ. He is Lord!

Why is that stressed?

It be may to ward off our becoming too familiar with a "Jesus" projected by our own sentimentality, to avoid our thinking Him as a "buddy" shaped in our own image, or imagining too "personal" an acquaintance with Him as a servant whose chief concern is our comfort. It may be to warn us that walking, talking, chatting with a "Jesus" of our own imaging is only communing with ourselves. It may be to prejudge plays, novels, musicals, songs that bring Jesus Christ to our level. Whatever the divine intent, the Creed does bring us up short with the reminder: <u>Jesus Christ is Lord!</u> He is Sovereign. He is King. He is highly exalted. Familiarity is impossible. Bowing before Him is obligatory, both here and hereafter.

How shall we translate that into the language of daily life? The omnipresent Lordship of Christ was the sobering strand, the origin of the "blue laws," the daily reminder of the seriousness of life that characterized the Puritans who made Western democracy.

Jesus Christ as Lord confronts us as God, capable of wrath, fierce anger, stern judgment.

Perhaps nothing more adequately accounts for the decline of Christian influence in the world than the confusion of the true Jesus Christ with the soft, sweet, sentimentalized image of Him so widely represented as ever-obliging "savior."

Yes, He came to save His people from their sins. John the Baptist said so. But yes, He does that only so the "saved" can unite as citizens of the Kingdom of God in history where obedience is rewarded and rebellion is condemned as route leading to hell. We play, as they say, for keeps. By act upon act we sculpt a soul, we paint a self-portrait, we serve God's or the Devil's purposes in history. And at the end, judgment is inevitable.

That's the way it is.

Let us think further on it: confessing Jesus Christ as Lord is for us also an awesome reminder that life is urgently serious business, the stakes eternal weal or woe. We may sing about Jesus, and theologize about Christ, but "Lord" freezes us in place: what now?

Now we recognize that the term "Lord" has a very special function in the Creed. Here is the point of transition between the Jesus who comes *"to seek and to save the lost"* (Luke 19:10), and the Jesus Christ who is coming as Judge, as the Creed will lead us to confess.

It is as Lord that Jesus Christ is both *"the Lamb of God who takes away the sin of the world"* (John 1:29), and the Lamb whose *"wrath"* at the end of time sends men great and small fleeing for cover (Rev. 6:15-17).

Consider a "wrathful" lamb! That is a contradiction in terms. Yet it exactly portrays the Son of God who is "accepted" as "Savior" but denied as Christ, only to be met as Lord. Nor is that beyond comprehension. How would a just Lord deal with those for whom He gave His own life when they deliberately flout the gift through declining the life of obedience which such sacrifice made possible?

It is in Jesus Christ as Lord that God *"commands everyone everywhere to repent,"* and by Jesus Christ as Lord that God *"will judge the world in righteousness"* (Acts 17:30-31). If there had been no incarnation, and if there had been no Calvary and no tomb--if the Son of God had not endured all this, well might we say that repentance is unnecessary or pass off obedience as out of our reach.

Or we might foolishly look to "Jesus" as paying for sin without demanding anything of us in return. But as "Lord," He makes such foolish sentimentality impossible.

The Bible makes ignorance itself a sin.

Through the Cross the Word goes out to all as Paul preached it to the Athenians: *"The times of ignorance God overlooked, but now he commands all people everywhere to repent because he has fixed a day on which he will judge the world in righteousness by a man whom he has appointed, and of this he has given assurance to all by raising him from the dead"* (Acts 17:30-31). He speaks of Jesus and of Christ as together Lord.

Our confession of the term "Lord" confirms upon us what the risen Christ says to His disciples in the Great Commission: *"All authority in heaven and on earth has been given to me..."* (Mat. 28:19).

True it is that the Lordship of Christ, so vivid to the eye of faith, is not now visible to the secular eye. *"As it is"* says the Epistle to the Hebrews, in something of an understatement, *"we do not yet see everything in subjection to him"* (Heb. 2:8). The natural eye sees almost the opposite, just a random world seething in unrest, violence and rebellion. Unbelief sees a Church convulsed by secular intrusion, a Word of God twisted into inconceivable dimensions by theological speculation, a sentimentality masqueraded as "love" that draws no lines, knows no law, indulges every disobedience, and sneers at the idea of damnation--despite the Cross!

Only through faith do we see that Jesus Christ is Lord at this very moment, and always. By faith we see that in the turmoil of the times the fundamental drama of existence is unfolding under divine providence, and that the Lord Jesus Christ is firmly at the helm of His world and of all history.

Because that company of the believing around the strait gate is small, and the throng around the broad gate is so large (Mat. 7:13-14), the voice of the few is easily drowned out by the volume of the many. No wonder that if we seek support in the popular press, in the fads and fashions of the times, in the certification of "science" or the authority of learning, we may feel dismally alone. If numbers counted, so we are.

But if we listen carefully (meaning willing to obey), the "still small voice" of the Word penetrates the tumult, drowns out the clamor, transcends the throng and keeps us on the "narrow way" which leads to life eternal.

Listen well!

By faith, through our "I believe" we engage in the struggle of the life of faith *"against the principalities, against the powers, against the world rulers of this present darkness, against the spiritual hosts of wickedness in the heavenly places"* (Eph. 6:12).

And we know that the struggle is never in vain: *"In all these things we are more than conquerors through him who loved us. For I am sure that neither death, nor life, nor angels, nor principalities, nor things present, nor things to come, nor powers, nor height, nor depth, nor anything else in all creation will be able to separate us from the love of God in Christ Jesus our Lord"* (Rom. 8:37-39).

Such certainty resides in the confession of Jesus Christ as "Lord."

Our "I believe" is not derived from, nor bolstered by, nor weakened through, reading the newspapers. The Lord reigns. Here faith rests secure.

The confession of Jesus Christ as "Lord" reminds us that there is a decisive "either/or" about Christianity, to use a title of a book by the Danish existentialist Soren Kierkegaard. There is a finality about His Word, despite the "scholars" who now handle it so casually and criticize so arrogantly. The Lord's biblical Word is going to be their, and our, Judge on that Last Day, as we shall soon confess.

Only as we more and more perceive that Jesus as Savior is not to be detached from Christ as Prophet/Priest/King, and both are summed up in confessing Him as Lord, will we understand why it was that He offended so many who heard Him. Indeed, so much offended them that on various occasions they wished to kill Him, and at last did so on the Cross.

It was Jesus Christ as Lord, all three "offices" together which brought Him to the Cross. He explains: *"If I had not come and spoken to them, they would not have sin; but now they have no excuse for their sin"* (John 15:22). His prophetic Word as Christ, spoken as Lord, at last led Him to execution by those who hated Him for what He said--as indeed they had hated the Prophets before Him.

Did they misunderstand Him? No, they understood Him well enough, as subversive to their way of life. He stripped the fig-leaves from their naked greed, lust, deceit, arrogance and most of all their hypocrisy. Forced to choose between faith with repentance, or unfaith with murder, those whose sins the Lord exposed chose murder. Then, and since!

Just what, we may ask, does the Lord mean by *"come and spoken to them..."*? Spoken what, say?

We think at once of the terrifying denunciations of the religious leadership of Israel reported in Matthew, chapter 23: *"Woe to you, scribes and Pharisees, hypocrites.... Woe to you, blind guides..."* followed by four repetitions of, *"Woe to you, scribes and Pharisees, hypocrites...."* (Mat. 23:13,16,23,25,27,29), each with its own indictment. These won Him no friends in high places.

Was it His saying that the narrow Way to life is so hard that few find and walk that road (Mat. 7:13)? We who prefer the easy way of raising a hand don't want to hear that.

Or was it His saying, *"If you believed Moses, you would believe me, for he wrote of me. But if you do not believe his writings, how will you believe my words?"* (John 5:46)?

When did Moses write of Jesus Christ? Paul tells us: *"Thus it is written, 'The first man Adam became a living being'; the last Adam became a life-giving spirit"* (I Cor. 15:45). Paul is quoting Genesis 2:7. In writing of the "first Adam" Moses writes of Jesus Christ, the "second Adam." Our Lord Himself confirms the parallel when He teaches, after His resurrection, the disciples He meets on the road to Emmaus: *"And beginning with Moses and all the prophets, he interpreted to them in all the scriptures the things concerning himself"* (Luke 24:27). In confirming the Genesis account of man's creation and fall, Jesus was finding Israel also guilty of depravity, a blindness which rendered them incapable of judging Him. In such "speaking to them," He exposed their own proclivity to sin, and they hated Him accordingly.

So does the modern mind which ridicules Genesis rather than accept Jesus' teaching.

Jesus obviously generated hatred in the Church of His day, among those who were more than satisfied with their religious life. It was they who persuaded Pilate to give Him over to execution. So today we are most threatened by the Lie masquerading as truth, subtly insinuated into the household of 'faith.' As the Lord Himself warns, *"And one's foes will be those of his own household"* (Mat. 10:36). The Church is always threatened from within.

The Creed inserts the "Our Lord" as a kind of "Puritan" emphasis, to impress upon us by way of our "I believe" the solemn character of Christianity, the stern and relentless pressure of obligation, to drive home our total dependence upon the authority of the Word.

It was the "Lord" who called those subversives labeled "heroes of faith" in the eleventh chapter of Hebrews to their costly witness. Their "I believe" no doubt led to heaven, but it is written of them that on the way, *"Some were tortured, refusing to accept release, that they might rise to a better life. Others suffered mocking and scourging, and even chains and imprisonment. They were stoned, they were sawn in two, they were killed with the sword; they went about in skins of sheep and goats, destitute, afflicted, ill-treated--of whom the world was not worthy--wandering over deserts and mountains, and in dens and caves of the earth"* (Heb. 11:35-38).

It is instructive, here also, to ask what it was that made these servants of God so obnoxious to their contemporaries? It can hardly have been offering "salvation" for the asking over a coffee-break. It could hardly have been acts of charity. Was it, for them, as it was for their Lord, and should be for us, their inflexible adherence to, and effort to obey, a Word which reveals the ways of depraved mankind to be evil? The Lord has no use for a pale, pallid, timid 'witness' which tailors Truth to the tastes of the times, to trends, to fads, or to the compulsion of influence or threat.

What does this mean for daily lives as ordinary as our own? What are we to learn from those victims of hatred?

Shall we say that for us the admonition is simply to know what we stand on, and to stand firm. Convictions will show. No need for display. No need for imposing ourselves upon others. Commitment to the Commandments will come out on the job, along the way, in the home, in stands we take on issues which affect the coming of the Kingdom on earth among us. Such will be our witness.

Interest in the Word, participation in the Church, devotion to public morality, dedication to social progress will have their effect, and mark us as citizens of His Kingdom.

We can now summarize our confession of the Second Person of the Holy Trinity:

1. As <u>Jesus</u> He saves "from" the guilt and penalty of sin, and "for" the life of obedience.

2. As <u>Christ</u> the Prophet He teaches us what "from" and what "for."

3. As <u>Christ</u> the Priest He intercedes for us with the Father when we falter along the way of attempted obedience.

4. As <u>Christ</u> the King He mandates walking in the light of His inspired Word, and protects us on our way.

5. As <u>Lord</u> He enters awesome authority and inescapable judgment into the drama of life.

6. And, as <u>Lord</u> He sends His Spirit to infuse His Word into the stuff of the believer's life. We will come to that.

"In the world," the Lord Jesus Christ teaches those who are subversive by reason of faith, *"you have tribulation; but be of good cheer, I have overcome the world"* (John 16:33).

Whatever temptation the world arouses, He has overcome. So can we!

Whatever opposition the world mounts, He has overcome. So can we!

In all things *"more than conquerors through him"* (Rom. 8:37). So we are!

Article 3.

WHO WAS CONCEIVED

BY THE HOLY SPIRIT,

BORN OF THE VIRGIN MARY

Let us observe that once again the Creed mirrors us to ourselves, and indeed acknowledge that here the Creed speaks as much of us as of Jesus Christ. If we truly confess the miraculous conception and birth of our Lord, we in the same breath admit that both were required by man's total incompetence to raise up a savior out of human stock alone. History records many "saviors," but the Virgin Birth indicts them all as counterfeit. And that, no doubt, is why both the miraculous conception and the miraculous birth are so widely repudiated now--"Who believes that virgin birth stuff any more?"

Well, they believe who see in the miracles how much we need them! They welcome the revelation of Jesus' conception and birth. The believer sees in the miraculous incarnation a divine certification of the extent of human depravity, including our own. Mankind's total inability to generate our own savior reveals our inherited limitations. In the light of the Incarnation we see the human race as victims of a blindness to truth and deafness to the Word that casts a shadow over all human competence as regards all the issues of history.

All speculation and every quibble over the miraculous conception and birth are undermined by the realization that the necessity of the divine miracle questions our ability to judge such things. What competence, we are taught, has a fallen mankind to question revelation at all?

The Virgin birth of our Lord demonstrates, to faith, into what abysmal darkness the Light of the miraculous had to come. Thanks to the events here confessed, *"The people who sat in darkness have seen a great light, and for those who sat in the region and shadow of death light has dawned"* (Mat. 4:16, quoting Is. 9:2). That's us.

It is worth bearing in mind that ideologies like Marxism, Fascism, Nazism and assorted lesser delusions all have one notion in common, namely that the human being can redeem, can reform, can refashion himself. The goal of ideologies is creation of a "new man." Soviet-educated Mikhail Heller details in his book The Formation Of Soviet Man, the deadly faith of Soviet theorists in the possibility of creating a new species of human being through the Marxist system. This misconception of human potential underlies the willingness of fanatics to pursue genocide as a quick way of clearing the decks of the "old" style human. Only to find that the tyrants whom the "system" puts in their place are the "old" man at his worst.

Our Lord's miraculous conception rules out any possibility of mankind's producing a "new man" on its own.

We who sat in darkness, the prophet says, have seen a great light. In that light we "see" <u>both</u> a darkness, and a Light, known only to belief. For it is characteristic of unbelief that it takes stumbling for perfect balance, and darkness for the light of Reason.

And what, then, does the believer "see"?

Our "I believe" acknowledges that there is something in man's natural descent which is repudiated by the God who makes and sustains us. Depraved humankind is unable to engender a savior, and God cannot use man's natural descent to incarnate His son. The "Son of Man," as Jesus was fond of calling Himself, must be brought to conception and birth outside the normal lineage of the sons of men. This is not divine prejudice, but inherited human debility.

Pause over it reflectively: Jesus Christ had to be conceived by the Holy Spirit because human generation, since the Fall, is not fitted to produce anyone who can be true Savior and Lord. And the Savior must be born of a virgin to escape inheriting the depravity which natural descent imposes upon all mankind. Those who dispute or decry these miracles only demonstrate just how necessary they were. It is to cure just such blindness that Jesus came the way God miraculously provided.

This is not simply for information. Through faith it drives home the awesome truth that depravity is so inherent in us that no scheme of self-recreation, no guru, no religion, no philosophy, no incantation, nothing man can do suffices to liberate us from the burden of inherited depravity in all its faceted incompetence.

This is why the confession of the virgin birth of our Lord meets with such scornful rejection. It indicts those who would sit in judgment upon it. When sober judgment is impossible, the alternative is violence. Christianity is forbidden a hearing in public education in every way possible to those who are judged by it. Christianity enjoys no recognition in public decision-making. It is brushed aside wherever some kind of "science" can be cited as authority.

The very mode chosen by God for the coming of His Son into His world invites those who can "see" in His Light to acknowledge the depravity He came to atone. And finds sinful those who prefer blindness.

"Are we also blind?" the Pharisees sneeringly ask Jesus, after His healing of the man born blind. Jesus answers, *"If you were blind, you would have no guilt; but now that you say, 'We see,' your guilt remains"* (John 9:40-41). They hated Him for that.

The mode of Jesus' incarnation illumines the mode of our own re-birth into the kingdom of God. Just as a virgin cannot naturally bring forth new life, so we by nature cannot regenerate ourselves.

As Jesus Christ had to be born miraculously into human history, so those who are to be liberated from the Devil's dominion through Jesus Christ must be re-born miraculously through the same Spirit to escape sin's tentacles: *"But to all who received him, who believed in his name, he gave power to become the children of God; who were born, not of blood nor of the will of the flesh nor of the will of man, but of God"* (John 1:12-13).

See God's cure for human incompetence in the miracle of Jesus' birth:

> Conceived by the Holy Spirit: revealing that Jesus Christ was truly God.

> Born of the Virgin Mary: revealing that Jesus Christ was truly man, but untainted by depravity.

Or again:

> To satisfy divine justice: truly God, conceived by the Holy Spirit.

> To do so for mankind: truly man, born of the Virgin Mary.

The so-called "modern mind" is arrogantly bent upon its own "independence." But how totally unaware that every exercise of that presumed independence to fling aside God's revelation only witnesses all the more to its incompetence, its preference to staying in the "darkness" which envelops all those outside the Light of revelation.

Mary was greeted by God's messenger, the angel Gabriel, with *"Hail, O favored one, the Lord is with you!"* She was *"greatly troubled at the saying, and considered in her mind what sort of greeting this might be."* Nor could the prospect of being an unwed mother in her time and place, as revealed by the angel, be anything but shocking. You should re-read and ponder the account in Luke 1:26-38.

Mary's answer, none-the-less, models for everyone, everywhere, the appropriate response to hearing the Word of God: *"Behold, I am the handmaid of the Lord; let it be to me according to your word"* (Luke 1:38). The believer hears in these words the antithesis to Eve's acquiescence to the word of the Devil in the Garden of Eden. For Eve, not Thy will but mine; for Mary, not my will but Thine.

Who of these two is your model?

Confession of the Virgin birth impresses upon us our need of the power of the same Spirit, using a Word from God, to renew life within us, and set us upon the way of obedience. For we, too, cannot engender new life. The Spirit must break into our lives on the vehicle of the Word to create the faith and to motivate the obedience which together form the new life. This is why the Creed will bring us to "I believe in the Holy Spirit," who is Author of our sanctification as He was of the conception of the Savior in whom justification is to be found.

Never mistake this facet of the Creed as leftover myth no longer acceptable in this "scientific" age. It is a confession of Truth of profound importance, both for what it reveals about the Son of God and about us.

Article 4.

SUFFERED UNDER

PONTIUS PILATE,

WAS CRUCIFIED,

DEAD, AND BURIED

And what's in this for us?

Much, of course, as with all the Creed, to our profit.

Let us recall that Rome ruled much of the known world at the time of Jesus. Pontius Pilate, Roman governor of Judea, represented Roman rule and Roman law in Jerusalem. Roman law is still regarded as having been among the best of its kind in equity and administration of justice.

So?

Well, as spokesman for this law, Pontius Pilate three times declared to those clamoring for Jesus' blood, *"I have found no cause for death in him"* (Luke 23:22). God uses Pilate to describe Jesus as God saw Him, and sees us in Him by faith.

The arrogant, and cowardly, Roman governor portrays all too obviously our own lapses in moral stamina. He yields to mob pressure: *"And so Pilate, wishing to satisfy the crowd...delivered Jesus, when he had scourged him, to be crucified"* (Mark 15:15).

The judge who finds Jesus guiltless is the very judge who delivers Him over to scourging. Pilate was traitor to his own law. Matthew reports that Pilate *"took water, and washed his hands before the multitude, saying, 'I am innocent of the blood of this just person; see to it yourselves'....and having scourged Jesus, delivered him to be crucified"* (Mat. 27:24). What awesome demonstration of human venality: he scourges Him whom he declares just, and dabbles in water to expiate blood! It is such water which, in baptism of faith, does indeed cleanse, but which in idle jest condemns the governor's blasphemy.

But bear in mind that in Pontius Pilate we have an exemplar of mankind as it is without faith. Still more, an exemplar of the kind of person we fall into being every time we betray our faith.

We are easily impressed by pomp and circumstance, especially as of the wealthy and the well-known. Let what we see of the powerful and ruthless governor of Judea show us that what matters about the acts of anyone and everyone is always the same: obedient to God's will or rebellious against it? Thus for the common good, or adverse to it? Be the act in a palace or a cottage, by rich or poor, by famous or unknown, the issue is ever the same: whose word governs?

How would Pilate have guessed that his cynical *"Behold the Man!"* (Ecce homo--John 19:5) forever speaks Truth to faith, for in Him was man fully to be found. And in this beaten, stricken, unglamorous and bloody Man we see ourselves as God, outside Christ, beholds us. How often, if not in words then in behavior, do we even now echo Pilate's sneering, *"What is truth?"* (John 18:38). Pilate not knowing that God had laid upon his lips Truth for all time by declaring Jesus without fault? How evident to those who believe: unwilling, unwitting Pontius Pilate, used like Balaam's ass (Num. 22-23), to voice revealed Truth!

All history reaches its climax there in Jerusalem, moving from the Judgment seat of Rome to the illegal execution on Calvary. The best law man could devise ordains and repeats the worst crime man could commit, the effort to drive God out of man's presence. Pilate's praetorium recalls the essence of the Fall in the Garden: get God out of man's way! Done by the "best" people, chiefs of the "Church" who manipulated the mob to secure their ends, and a chief of state with no backbone to match his authority.

It is instructive that learned historian Oswald Spengler, author of the Decline Of The West, sees in the confrontation of Pilate by Jesus also the pinnacle of human history, but in his own terms. Two forms of social organization, for Spengler, met there in Jerusalem, the creative, youthful "culture" of Jesus versus the rigid, dying "civilization" of the Roman empire. It is a model, Spengler thought, of the modern situation where the West is dying because today's civilization is strangling culture in the lifeless grasp of science and technology. Spengler lacks the revealed perspective, but he is correct in sensing the centrality of that encounter.

The event does set before us something of a sobering choice among frailties: are we more like the Roman Governor who judges Jesus innocent and then, for fear of the people, has Him scourged and delivered to death? Are we, too, moral victims of public opinion and the latest faddisms? Like the mob which mindlessly shouted "Crucify him!" because everyone else did? Or like the very fickle ones who may have cried out "Hosanna" on the first Palm Sunday and "Crucify Him!" on the first Good Friday? Or like the high priests who out of envy manipulated Pilate through mobocracy? Or like the Pharisees who hated Him for exposing their hypocrisy? Or, in fact, like them all, more of one today, and of the other tomorrow? Which are you?

Do we want to know why even the best laid schemes of mankind "gang oft agley"? See how far off the path of justice the best made system of human law went on that first Good Friday morning! It's just what "conceived by the Holy Spirit, born of the Virgin Mary" teach us: not even the best mankind can do escapes the terrible taint of sin and depravity. Roman law fails in the pinch.

Crucified:

Crucifixion was in itself a uniquely cruel form of execution. It was also symbol of a unique rejection: signifying repudiation by mankind off whose world the victim is raised, and repudiation by heaven, which the victim does not reach. It is a reminder that "man is homeless under the sun."

In the symbolism of the Cross is revealed our own natural status, save for justification by faith through the death of Jesus. Earth cannot be our enduring abode; death intervenes. Heaven rejects us until God be reconciled to us through the "I believe" in the Truth summarized by the Creed. In the Cross we perceive the depth of our depravity, the extent of our need, the divine condemnation of our guilt and disobedience--and the incalculable significance of divine grace.

Not by accident, a cross, to be a cross, unites a vertical and horizontal member. The vertical speaks of God and heaven; the horizontal of man and history. In the Cross of Christ the horizontal and vertical are reconciled in the death of Him who gave His life upon it: *"For in him the fullness of God was pleased to dwell, and through him to reconcile to himself all things, whether on earth or in heaven, making peace by the blood of the cross"* (Col. 1:19-20).

Jesus the Christ makes the Cross of Calvary a model for the self-sacrifice required of all who would walk in His Word: *"Then Jesus told his disciples, 'If any one would come after me, let him deny himself and take up his cross and follow me'"* (Mat. 16:24), *"by which,"* as St. Paul puts it, *"the world has been crucified to me, and I to the world"* (Gal. 6:14).

This must be the lesson of the mode of Jesus' execution for us. Just as He gave His life as sacrifice upon a cross as Highpriest of our redemption, so He calls upon us to sacrifice our self-interest as the priesthood of believers to which we are called.

Taking up our cross simply implies that we deny ourselves in obedience to His Word, as He denied Himself in obedience to His Father's Word.

Dead:

The Cross rises not only at the center of world history, but at the center of each person's history. If our sins are through faith atoned on the Cross of Jesus Christ, then we are shouldering daily our own cross of self-sacrifice in the freedom of obedience. If the cross of self-sacrifice is not our life-style, then the Cross of Calvary is not our atonement, and then our end will be the condemnation which Calvary symbolized.

Death both physical and spiritual is the divine penalty upon sin: *"..for in the day you eat of it [the forbidden fruit] you shall die"* (Gen. 1:17). Christ undergoes this penalty upon the Cross for all who are united with Him through faith. It is our "I believe" that certifies in the self this liberating union with our Lord.

Jesus dies physically, and thus leads the way for all who believe through the valley of the shadow: *"Yea, though I walk through the valley of the shadow of death, I fear no evil, for thou art with me, thy rod and thy staff, they comfort me"* (Ps. 23:4). He was there before us, and is there when we approach.

He dies spiritually, that is by a mysterious alienation from God, the very Source of life, as revealed in His agonizing cry from the Cross: *"My God, my God, why hast thou forsaken me?"* (Mat. 27:46). In Him, through our "I believe," is our alienation from God both affirmed, suffered and overcome.

Let us take note, that *"the second death"* (Rev. 20:14, 21:8) waits upon all who decline *"to hear his voice...as long as it is called 'today'"* (Heb. 3:15,13).

Buried:

Yes, we confess it as proof that Jesus Christ indeed was dead.

The tomb is the final and inexorable reminder of the penalty laid by God upon the Fall: *"In the sweat of your face you shall eat bread till you return to the ground, for out of it you were taken; you are dust, and to dust you shall return"* (Gen. 3:19). In the grave, foretold in Genesis, culminates the effect of the Fall and its consequences. The tomb certifies the truth of Genesis.

Ah, but Christ's brief tenure there relieves us of the grave's grim menace! For those whose "I believe" opens themselves to the Word, the Lord's burial makes the tomb a way-station en route to heaven, a vestibule to life eternal.

Article 5.

HE DESCENDED INTO HELL;

THE THIRD DAY

HE ROSE FROM THE DEAD

The "I believe" commits us to recognition that there is a hell. What and where we do not know, but that we confess. There is a place of total and unending alienation from God with all the suffering that implies. We are foreclosed from joining intellectuals who speculate that hell is an ancient, outmoded conception, an impossibility. No one speaks more often and more threateningly of hell than does Jesus Christ Himself, as, say: *"And do not fear those who kill the body but cannot kill the soul; rather fear him who can destroy both soul and body in hell"* (Mat. 10:28, so also in Mat. 5:22, 25:41, Mark 9:47-48, Luke 12:5, 18:23, etc.).

Hell surely implies the complete antithesis of all that for which each of us is made, the total un-manning of man. Hell implies bondage to the Devil in unending torment. Thus Jesus portrays it: *"...at the close of the age, the Son of Man will send his angels, and they will gather out of his kingdom all causes of sin and evildoers, and throw them into the furnace of fire; there men will weep and gnash their teeth"* (Mat. 13:41-42).

Believers escape hell's clutches only because the Lord vicariously suffered all the condemnation due us by our own inheritance and misbehavior.

From the Cross Jesus cried, *"'It is finished,'"* St. John reports, *"and bowed his head and gave up the spirit"* (John 19:30).

Interpreters have, therefore, been divided as to what the Creed means to impress upon us by "descended into hell."

We will reflect further upon that phrase in a moment. For now, don't casually pass by the import of this Article of the Creed.

Consider how common it is among "with-it" theologians to assert their having come of age by pooh-poohing the idea of hell as incompatible with a "loving God."

We have observed already that the very incarnation of God's love, Jesus the Christ, speaks more often of hell than any other of those whose Word composes the Holy Scriptures. There is no incompatibility between divine love and divine rejection of those who reject that love. And what could the consequence of such rejection be but hell?

It is not as if God had designed a kind of Gulag for rebels. God just cannot extend to unbelief the joy of His presence. To be banished from God, after the possibility of reconciliation has ended in death, is hell. Jesus' favorite metaphor for the pain of hell is *"weeping and gnashing of teeth"* (Mat. 8:12, 13:42, Luke 13:28, etc.). Opportunity rejected; endless alienation.

If our confession of "descended into hell" implies a part of the Lord's suffering, which He declares finished while still on the Cross, then His descent into hell must be understood as included in the torments endured before His death. This is a common conception, recorded for example in the Heidelberg Catechism (Q/A 44).

If, as the Creed seems to imply, the descent into hell followed after the completion of His suffering, then we here confess that our Lord entered hell, not as victim but as Victor. This, too, has been taught in the Church, especially in Catholicism. Hell itself was "harrowed," that is entered and despoiled by a triumphant Lord who thus validates His liberation from hell's grasp of all who believe.

Thanks to His triumphal entry, the threat of hell hovers no more over the future of all whose "I believe" opens their lives to the power of His Word and Spirit. The risen Lord shatters hell's thrall.

This view is vividly depicted by the poet Dante in Book I of his Divine Comedy, entitled The Inferno. Dante describes in words he assigns to the pagan poet Virgil, who for Dante was in Limbo, how the triumphant Christ crashed the gate to release from the precincts of hell the souls of the Old Testament saints held in Limbo until the triumphant One should come. The very citadel of the Adversary who gained a foothold in history in man's Fall was itself entered and despoiled by the Victor who had earned by His self-sacrifice the Father's authority to do so. Jesus may have made oblique reference to this "harrowing" in saying, *"Or how can one enter a strong man's house and plunder his goods, unless he first binds the strong man?"* (Mat. 12:29).

In our confession of the reality of hell, implying the reality of the Devil and his angels also, we at the same time rise to confession of the triumphal conquest of Devil and hell in Jesus Christ our Lord. Denial of hell, dismissal of the Devil as old-fashioned mythology, offers no real liberation from the threat of these. Only through faith in the atoning sacrifice of Jesus Christ, only through devotion to an obedient life of good works, do we both recognize the reality of sin, of evil, of demons and eternal punishment and at the same time transcend them. Of the world, the flesh and the Devil we may say with our Savior, *"But be of good cheer, I have overcome the world"* (John 16:33).

Having thus displayed His victory over death and the Devil, the Christ fulfills the Psalmist's prediction: *"Thou hast ascended on high, thou hast led captivity captive"* (Ps. 68:18, quoted by Paul in Ephesians 4:8). Captivity--our captivity to the Devil--taken captive by our Lord, thus liberating all who believe as Israel was liberated from Egypt. The risen Lord demonstrates that there is no enemy free of His dominion: *"For I am persuaded,"* Paul says, *"that neither death, nor life, nor angels, nor principalities, nor things present, nor things to come, nor powers, nor height, nor depth, nor anything else in all creation, will be able to separate us from the love of God in Christ Jesus our Lord"* (Rom. 8:38-39).

Our Lord Himself says: *"I have the keys of Death and Hades"* (Rev. 1:18). These, then, were used in His "descent into hell," bursting open its grip on all who through faith are one with Him.

Without trying to determine which theological interpretation of this affirmation of the Creed accords best with revelation, we may receive strength and inspiration from the note of sovereign authority which the Creed conveys. Nothing, and no one, can impede the march triumphant of the saving and redeeming Lord. Neither His passage into our flesh, nor His suffering which followed, nor His death, nor His enduring either the torments or the actual environment of hell--<u>nothing</u> at all could block His way from heaven through complete Self-sacrifice on into complete redemption of all those united to Him in faith.

This we gladly confess. In this we find courage and hope inexhaustible.

Paul sings of it, as can we: *"Death is swallowed up in victory. O death, where is thy victory? O grave, where is thy sting?"* (I Cor. 15:54-55).

Resurrection bursts into human history.

"He is not here; he is risen!"

These are the words of the angel to the startled women who came early to the tomb (Mark 16:6).

We are surprised at their surprise. Did the disciples and those others close to Jesus not know? Had He not told them? Or was it rather a miracle so stupendous that we are the ones who sin in not standing perpetually in awe at this incomprehensible event: He arose from the dead! Precursor of our own rising. Death is not the end!

The risen Lord chastens those who had known Him best for their sluggish belief: *"'O foolish men, and slow of heart to believe all that the prophets have spoken! Was it not necessary that the Christ should suffer these things and enter into his glory?' And beginning with Moses and all the prophets, he interpreted to them in all the scriptures the things concerning himself"* (Luke 24:25-26).

And what is He even now thinking of you, and of us all, as He knows the state of our faith and assurance?

We do well, often, to echo the words of the disciples, *"Lord, increase our faith!"* (Luke 17:5).

One of the disciples, Thomas, forever blessedly known as "doubting Thomas" (how like ourselves!) misses the risen Lord's first appearance to His disciples and at first declines to believe in his Lord's resurrection: *"Unless I see in his hands the print of the nails, and place my hand in his side..."* (John 20:25). When next He appears to His disciples, the Lord most graciously accedes to Thomas' needs: *"Put your finger here, and see my hands; and put out your hand, and place it in my side; do not be faithless, but believing."* Thomas is overwhelmed by conviction: *"My Lord and my God!"* Then Jesus speaks infinite promise to all whose "I believe" suffers the doubts, sometimes, of Thomas' experience: *"Blessed are those who have not seen and yet believe"* (John 20:29). That's for you, and for us all who believe. Rejoice in it!

He is **NOT** here. The grave could not hold Him. Nor, thanks to Him, can it hold us.

He is **RISEN**. So shall we be!

St. Paul argues from life renewed in the resurrection to life at its source, our Lord's divinity: *"Who was declared the Son of God with power by the resurrection from the dead..."* (Rom. 1:4).

The presumed wisest in Athens, lacking faith, would not bow before it: *"And when they heard of the resurrection of the dead, some mocked, and others said, 'We will hear you again about this'"* (Acts 18:32). Athens, intellectual capitol of the ancient world, mocks what a child can receive in humble believing. Jesus speaks of it for our benefit: *"Truly, I say to you, whoever does not receive the kingdom of God like a child shall not enter it"* (Mark 10:15). See how limited the horizons of the "learned;" how long the shadow of the Fall; how gracious the Lord God to us who can say, "I believe...."

All roads, everyone's road, wends at last to the tomb. So we all know, and in uneasy contemplation, dread. But through our "I believe," the Lord's resurrection makes of the grave, as already observed, a portal, a way-station. The King of Glory (Ps. 24:7,9) has gone through, and all mankind follows in His train. Those whose "I believe" gives access to His Spirit leap through the tomb into life eternal. Those who do not believe pass from the tomb through resurrection to the *"second death"* (Rev. 20:14; 21:8).

Resurrection crowns the <u>via dolorosa</u> of Jesus' incarnation, suffering and death. The last Word, like the first, in Christianity is Life: *"I am the resurrection and the life,"* Jesus says to Martha, *"he who believes in me, though he die, yet shall he live, and whoever lives and believes in me shall never die."* And He adds, to us also, *"Do you believe this?"* (John 11:25-26).

Paul speaks for us, *"But in fact Christ has been raised from the dead, the first fruits of those who have fallen asleep. O grave where is thy victory? O death, where is thy sting?"* (I Cor. 15:19,17,20, 55).

"God raised him up," St. Peter says in the first post-Easter sermon, on Pentecost, *"having loosed the pangs of death, because it was not possible for him to be held by it"* (Acts 2:24).

The Psalmist speaks prophetically of the rising sun as being *"like a bridegroom coming out of his chamber, rejoicing like a young man to run a race"* (Ps. 19:5)--a daily symbol of the risen Lord emerging from His tomb, blazing a path of indubitable hope for our "I believe."

As Peter goes on to say, still quoting from the Psalmist in the Pentecostal sermon: *"Therefore did my heart rejoice, and my tongue was glad; moreover my flesh shall rest in hope, because thou wilt not leave my soul in hades, neither wilt thou allow thine Holy One to see corruption"* (Acts 2:26-27). Spoken prophetically of Jesus Christ, this Easter hope lives in each one who believes.

The resurrection unites us with a living host: *"So then you are no longer strangers and sojourners, but you are fellow citizens with the saints and members of the household of God, built upon the foundation of the apostles and prophets, Christ Jesus himself being the cornerstone, in whom the whole structure is joined together and grows into a holy temple in the Lord; in whom you also are built into it for a dwelling place of God in the Spirit"* (Eph. 2:19-22).

The resurrection frees us from the melancholy tyranny of fleeting time. Theologians speak in polysyllables of "proleptic" or "realized" eschatology. They mean that in the light streaming from the empty tomb we may live already in the great dawn which opens upon the new heaven and new earth. And so, without their esoteric terminology, we can do by faith.

There's persistent motivation in it. In our Lord's resurrection we are provided an incentive to the life of believing obedience.

As the Word of resurrection lays hold of us and our behavior: *"...let us lay aside every weight, and sin which clings so closely, and let us run with perseverance the race that is set before us, looking to Jesus the author and finisher of our faith, who for the joy that was set before him, endured the cross, despising the shame, and is set down at the right hand of the throne of God"* (Heb. 12:1-2).

Thanks to His resurrection the prophecy sounds the note of hope: *"For since the beginning of the world men have not heard, nor perceived by the ear, neither has the eye seen, O God, beside thee, what has been prepared for him who waits on God"* (Is. 64:4; quoted by St. Paul, I Cor. 2:9).

For believers like ourselves!

Article 6.

HE ASCENDED INTO HEAVEN, AND SITS ON THE RIGHT HAND OF GOD THE FATHER ALMIGHTY

The story is told simply enough.

The disciples are with Jesus, probably on a hillside near Jerusalem, and *"As they were looking on, he was lifted up, and a cloud took him out of their sight. And as they were gazing into heaven as he went, behold, two men stood by them in white robes, and said, 'Men of Galilee, why do you stand looking into heaven? This Jesus, who was taken up from you into heaven, will come in the same way as you saw him go into heaven.' Then they returned to Jerusalem..."* (Acts 1:9-12).

By faith we are there. We see Him raised; we return to the day's living refreshed, in strength renewed, and rejoicing.

Ascension means Jesus Christ's, the God/man Jesus Christ's, assumption of total Lordship. In our flesh, He is there: *"All authority in heaven and on earth has been given to me"* (Mat. 28:18). The Bible calls it His sitting *"on the right hand of God"* (Col. 3:1). Theologians speak of His "session" in heaven. The divine sovereignty is clothed in grace. God rules His creation through the agency of the Son incarnate in human flesh on man's behalf. There could be no better news for all who believe. Christ Jesus rules! Let believers rejoice and unbelievers tremble.

Notice: Jesus Christ came as Savior. He lived, suffered, died and rose to be Savior.

Notice also: Jesus Christ came as Prophet/Priest/King. He lived, suffered, died and rose to be Prophet/Priest/King, or say Teacher, Mediator, Master so that the liberated believer might know, and through the Spirit be empowered to do, the will of God in daily life.

Notice finally: as Jesus and Christ together He came as Lord. As Lord He ascended to exercise all authority in heaven and on earth at the right hand of His Father.

The message of the Church comes full circle in the confession of the Creed in our Lord and Savior. As in his sermon at Athens, Paul climaxes his preaching with the resurrection, the ascension and the impending final judgment.

The story which begins before the worlds were made, which takes visible form in the creation, which falls into shadow with man's defection, wends its way through law and prophecy to the incarnation, the suffering, death, burial, invasion of hell, resurrection and ascension of our Lord Jesus Christ. So briefly summarized, so infinite in Light, Power and Hope!

Yes, rejoice!

111

From heaven He teaches us via His Word; from thence He pleads for us in our trespasses against His Word; from thence He rules as King among all believers by the scepter of His Word (Calvin). From thence He keeps vigilant watch over His Church, guiding and warning and encouraging and when necessary threatening, as illustrated in the letters to the seven churches recorded in Revelation, chapters 2 and 3. From thence He blesses, and chastens, governing the discipling of believers. Be sure that you are among those daily learning better to hear and do this life-giving Word.

The inspired　Psalmist celebrates, in Words echoing down the centuries of the Church's pilgrimage, our Lord's triumphal return to heaven in His ascension: *"Lift up your heads, O ye gates! and be ye lifted up, ye everlasting doors! That the King of glory may come in! Who is the King of glory? The Lord, strong and mighty, the Lord, mighty in battle! Lift up your heads, O ye gates! and be ye lifted up, ye everlasting doors ! That the King of glory may come in. Who is this King of glory? The Lord of hosts, he is the King of glory!"* (Ps. 24:8-10).

The Lord returns to the Father, victor over the Devil, sin and the grave. But His work is not finished. If all we have confessed so far in the Creed were the full story, then the Exodus of Israel would have ended with escape through the Red Sea, and Paul's majestic treatise to the Romans could end with the fifth chapter: *"Therefore, being justified by faith, we have peace with God through our Lord Jesus Christ"* (Rom. 5:1).

But, the ascension declares that our liberation through faith is not the end of the Christian life, but the beginning. And, the Savior who freed us from bondage to sin, self and Devil not only liberates us to seek obedience but rules at the helm of the universe to make that search fruitful.

In Him, and by the indwelling of His Spirit, we sacramentalize the creation through obedient use of all that God provides.

And all this includes our flesh. We have noted that God provides for the unity of the human blood stream and unity of human stock by making Eve out of Adam's rib. Human flesh is one: *"He has made of one blood every nation of men to live on all the face of the earth"* (Acts 17:26).

It is our flesh which Jesus assumed from the Virgin Mary. It is our flesh that He carried by ascension into heaven. It is our flesh in which He chose to be incarnate which He has taken *"into the inner shrine behind the curtain, where Jesus has gone as forerunner on our behalf"* (Heb. 6:19-20). Why not give your arm a joyous pinch? That arm will one day be raised to life eternal where our Savior has now gone as "forerunner" for us.

The ascension is another step in our redemption. It stresses that what we do with freedom so hard-won by Jesus will now determine our eternal destiny. So Paul writes in his great Epistle on Christian liberty, to the Galatians: *"For you were called to freedom, brethren; only do not use your freedom as an opportunity for the flesh, but through love be servants of one another. For the whole of the law is summed up in one word, 'You shall love your neighbor as yourself'"* (Gal. 5:13-14). What this means for our daily living is what the Christian life is all about, what the Bible comes to teach us, and what the Spirit is given to make possible.

The Lord's ascension obtains for believers the indispensable indwelling presence of the Holy Spirit: *"Nevertheless I tell you the truth:"* Jesus says to His disciples in bidding them farewell, *"it is to your advantage that I go away, for if I do not go away, the Counselor will not come to you; but if I go, I will send him to you"* (John 16:7).

"I go to prepare a place for you," Jesus had said, *"and if I go to prepare a place for you, I will come again to receive you unto myself, that where I am there you may be also"* (John 14:2). How comfortable the ascension! How vibrant with hope!

Confession of belief in the ascension places us under obligation: *"If then you have been raised with Christ, seek the things that are above, where Christ is, seated at the right hand of God. Set your minds on things that are above, not on things that are on earth. For you have died, and your life is hid with Christ in God. When Christ who is our life appears, then you also will appear with him in glory"* (Col. 3:1-4).

Here our "I believe" admits the Word which braces us for the stress and storms of life as well as for all its challenges and opportunities. Our Savior is at the helm of the universe, engaged not only in cosmic control but involved in the minutest details of our lives--as Lord and Master. For the believer an inexhaustible source of great confidence, strength, and comfort: walk tall, speak truth, do His will, for the Lord reigns! For mankind, the source of both incalculable natural blessings, and too often unheeded spiritual warnings in natural disaster.

The Creed thus impresses through the "I believe" what the risen Lord anticipates by telling His disciples: *"All authority in heaven and on earth has been given to me"* (Mat. 28:18). To self-denying obedience, immeasurable assurance; to self-indulgent disobedience, immeasurable threat.

It was foretold by the Prophet Daniel: *"I saw in the night vision, and behold, with the clouds of heaven there came one like a son of man, and he came to the Ancient of Days and was presented before him. And to him was given dominion and glory and kingdom, that all peoples, nations, and languages should serve him; his dominion is an everlasting dominion, which shall not pass away, and his kingdom one that shall not be destroyed"* (Dan. 7:13-14).

Jesus' fondness for speaking of Himself as the "Son of Man" opens the eye of those who truly hear Him to this dimension of the Man who looked to the natural eye as merely an itinerant teacher. To the crowds of Jerico, for example, the teacher passing by was just "Jesus of Nazareth," but to blind Bartimaeus, the beggar, illumined by the Spirit, the man passing by was *"Jesus, Thou Son of David.."* And the beggar could ask, *"have mercy on me!"* (Mark 10:46-7).

So can we...beggars.

There are two sides, as usual, to this confessed Truth:

1)   On the one hand, we know by faith that our Savior exercises absolute authority in heaven and on earth. He can say, and we do believe Him: *"Let not your heart be troubled; believe in God, believe also in me"* (John 14:1). St. Paul can triumphantly declare: *"If God is for us, who is against us? He who did not spare his own Son but gave him up for us all, will he not also give us all things with him? Who shall bring any charge against God's elect? It is God who justifies; who is to condemn? It is Christ Jesus who died, yes, who was raised from the dead, who is at the right hand of God, who indeed intercedes for us."* And because this is so, Paul can go on to assert, for himself and for us, as we have already heard: *"For I am sure that neither death, nor life, nor angels, nor principalities, nor power, nor height, nor depth, nor anything else in all creation, will be able to separate us from the love of God in Christ Jesus our Lord"* (Rom. 8:38-39).

2)   On the other hand, the risen Lord is on record: *"Not every one who says to me, 'Lord, Lord,' shall enter the kingdom of heaven, but he who does the will of my Father who is in heaven"* (Mat. 7:21). Only the obedient genuinely enjoy in the present the joy of citizenship in the Lord's Kingdom.

The Lord of all the earth sits at the right hand of God the Father, to exercise all authority in heaven and on earth by way of His Word, truly preached, heard, obeyed. That Word is, we are told: *"living and active, sharper than any two-edged sword, piercing to the division of soul and spirit, of joints and marrow, and discerning the thoughts and intentions of the heart. And before him no creature is hidden, but all are open and laid bare to the eyes of him with whom we have to do"* (Heb. 4:12-13).

We rejoice in, and at the same time stand in awe of, our confession: He ascended into heaven....

Article 7.

FROM THENCE

HE SHALL COME TO JUDGE

THE LIVING AND THE DEAD

The ascended Lord is not going to remain in heaven. How urgent, therefore, it is that all who think they believe pay close attention to Paul's admonition: *"Examine yourselves, to see whether you are holding to your faith. Test yourselves"* (II Cor. 13:5). Some methods for such testing are revealed in the Letters to the seven churches given for delivery to St. John in chapters two and three of Revelation. Read them, reflect upon and apply them to yourselves.

It was predicted at Jesus' ascension: *"This Jesus, who was taken up from you into heaven, will come in the same way as you saw him go into heaven.'"* (Acts 1:9-12). This was said after, in His ascending, *"a cloud took him out of their sight"* (v.9). He leaves the world hidden by a cloud; His second coming will be on the clouds: *"Then will appear the sign of the Son of man in heaven, and then all the tribes of the earth will mourn, and they will see the Son of man coming on the clouds of heaven with power and great glory"* (Mat. 24:30). Again, before the high priest, Jesus says, *"But I tell you, hereafter you will see the Son of man seated at the right hand of Power, and coming on the clouds of heaven"* (Mat. 26:64). The high priest called that "blasphemy." The believer hears it as awesome prophecy.

It will not be another "Christmas," then? With angels singing, and shepherds and wise men marveling?

No, not that way. Not at all that way: *"Behold, he is coming with the clouds, and every eye will see him, every one who pierced him; and all tribes of the earth will wail on account of him"* (Rev. 1:7).

Why wailing? Because the "today" for hearing the Gospel is past, and the time of judgment is at hand.

The "Second Coming" adds an urgency to the passing of time, not only to our own brief, fleeting moment, but to time itself. There is an end in view, for each finite life and for the universe and for the time which seems so swiftly bearing us along. An end culminating in Judgment.

Jesus Himself describes it: *"When the Son of Man comes in his glory, and all the angels with him, then he will sit on his glorious throne. Before him will be gathered all the nations, and he will separate them one from another as a shepherd separates the sheep from the goats, and he will place the sheep at his right hand, but the goats at the left. Then the King will say to those on his right hand, 'Come, O blessed of my Father, inherit the kingdom prepared for you from the foundation of the world.... Then he will say to those at his left hand, 'Depart from me, you cursed, into the eternal fire prepared for the Devil and his angels... "* (Mat, 25:31-34; 41).

How different this anticipation is from the joy on the hills of Bethlehem on that first Christmas eve. There the song of angels, and foretold here the wailing of unbelief; there the *"Fear not"* (Luke 2:10), and here the shrieks of terror.

Can it be the same Jesus?

Yes, He is the same, and this no doubt explains why, after His resurrection, Jesus Christ did not show Himself to Pilate, nor to the Priests who brought Him to Pilate, nor to the mob who shouted, "Crucify him" on instigation of their blind leadership. He knew what they all did not want to know: we will meet again!

That is the future for everyone, believer and unbeliever alike. He will meet us on that Last Day.

The Last Judgment sets Christianity in an awesome light. Belief or unbelief, obedience or rebellion come to fruition at last. The world is destined to judgment, before the throne of Him who suffered and died at the world's hands, not only in Jerusalem but who suffers wherever and whenever He is scorned or ignored. The face of each moment of our lives has another side: it will re-appear for judgment. The book of life being written by each of us now will be opened for scrutiny before the Lord: *"And the dead were judged by what was written in the books"* (Rev. 20:12), those books which each of us is writing with the pen of time.

Imagine the shock which would have benumbed Pilate, casually discussing with his friends "What is truth?" over fine wine and in luxurious surroundings, to discover that on the Last Day he would be met by the Galilean he had done to unjust death, then standing as Judge of all the earth, Pilate and cronies included. And what a sobering revelation for each of us: "From thence He shall come to judge the living and the dead."

Victim of his unbelief, Pilate foolishly shrugged off his responsibility to Truth by washing his hands in water, unwittingly mimicking baptism. But how easily are we tempted to shrug off our responsibility for the obedient life by as casually thinking to wash our hands in His shed blood. Because we are under grace, we might foolishly suppose, we are exempted from the divine Law. But we are as mistaken as was Pilate if we imagine that because we are indeed liberated by Calvary from guilt and from bondage to the Devil and self-indulgence, we can ignore self-denial in obedience to the divine commandments for which we are set free. Judgment as surely awaits this mistake as it does Pilate's.

"Think not, " Jesus tells us, *"that I have come to abolish the law and the prophets* [but there are some who do think just that!]*; I have not come to abolish them but to fulfil them. And truly, I say to you, till heaven and earth pass away, not an iota, not a dot, will pass from the law until all is accomplished"* (Mat. 5:17-18).

We have, of course, heard this theme sounding in the Creed all along.

By faith we grasp more and more the import of the Truth that to us, as to Pilate, to the false priests, to the mob, to rebels of all times, to the self-deceived within the Church and the self-satisfied without, the promise of Jesus Christ as Judge is the same: *"...and I will give to each of you as your works deserve"* (Rev. 3:23).

We find ourselves included when speaking to *"His disciples first,"* St. Luke reports, Jesus issues a frightening warning: *"I tell you, my friends, do not fear those who kill the body, and after that have no more they can do. But I will warn you whom to fear; fear him who, after he has killed, has power to cast into hell; yes, I tell you, fear him!"* (Luke 12:4-5).

Faith obliges us to ask: of whom is the Lord speaking here? "Fear" whom? As "friends" of Jesus?

We may on first thought suppose that Jesus the Savior will most certainly protect us from just this threatening Power, whoever it turns out to be. But who, then, is this fearsome Person, against whom Jesus is warning, not His enemies but His "friends"?

Is it the Devil who has the power *"to cast into hell"*? No, that will be the fate of the Devil himself (Rev. 20:10). He certainly will not be the judge of mankind on the Last Day.

Our "I believe" permits no other alternative: this fearsome Person, of whom the Lord warns His disciples to beware, is Jesus Himself. We know that because the risen and ascended Lord tells St. John: *"...I have the keys of Death and Hades"* (Rev. 1:17-18). I have the keys of Death and Hades! He is the one who can cast into hell!

Jesus Himself will not underwrite the fantasy which pictures Him as the meek, mild, loving Savior whose only concern is for our security and happiness. There is indeed the loving side to our Savior, love enough to die for His own. But the very fact that He has sacrificed Himself on our behalf emerges in His demand that we likewise sacrifice ourselves in obedience to Him. And when we misconstrue the urgency of that demand, or think it need not apply to those who believe, then we find ourselves confronted by a Judge who has, and uses, the keys to Death and Hades. Divine love, Augustine says, either warms in its light or burns in its judgment, leads to heaven or casts into hell.

"I will warn you whom to fear...!"

Remember!

And what is this "fear" of which the Lord warns us?

Terror of judgment and condemnation is obviously implied, followed by fear of banishment to hell. Yes, we are to fear that so much that obedience seems light and easy by comparison.

This, then, becomes a redemptive "fear" leading to a life that will pass judgment at the end: *"Fear God, and keep his commandments; for this is the whole duty of man. For God will bring every deed into judgment, with every secret thing, whether good or evil"* (Eccles. 12:13-14).

The believer, then, is warned as a "friend," by our Savior and Lord to fear the Lord Jesus Christ Himself!

The Lord Jesus Christ is saying to His "friends" fear Me! And He continues His discourse to treat by parable of the Judgment Day, saying, *"And that servant who knew his master's will, but did not make ready or act according to his will, shall receive double lashes....Every one to whom much is given, of him will much be required"* (Luke 12:47,48).

How much will be required of us to whom the Apostles Creed and all it implies of the Bible is graciously provided?

It is He who *"will judge the world with righteousness, and the peoples with equity"* (Ps. 98:9). And He has the power to save and the power to cast into hell.

Yes, the warning is urgent. Christianity is no game, no cornucopia of freebies. It is life or death.

It is of Jesus as Judge that the Psalmist prophesied, *"I will tell of the decree of the Lord: He said to me, 'You are my son, today I have begotten you. Ask of me, and I will make the nations your heritage, and the ends of the earth your possession. You shall break them with a rod of iron, and dash them in pieces like a potter's vessel.'"*

And then the Psalmist addresses the leaders of mankind, in words meant for us all: *"Now therefore, O kings, be wise; be warned, O rulers of the earth. Serve the Lord with fear, with trembling, kiss the Son, lest he be angry, and you perish in the way; for his wrath is quickly kindled. Blessed are all who take refuge in him"* (Ps. 2:7-11).

Jesus Christ, the only begotten Son, is He whom the wise will fear by obedience. It is of Himself that He says: *"...who has the key of David, who opens and no one shall shut, who shuts and no one opens"* (Rev. 3:7).

The transition implied in the ascension is completely impressed upon us now. He whose self-sacrifice liberates mankind from bondage to the Devil, making possible the freedom realized through obedience to His Word, is the same One who warns repeatedly that abuse of the liberation He has earned destines the disobedient to the place *"where there will be weeping and gnashing of teeth"* (Mat. 8:12; 13:42,50; 22:13, etc.).

John the Baptist introduces Jesus, saying: *"Behold, the Lamb of God, who takes away the sin of the world!"* (John 1:29). John the Apostle reveals the same Jesus at the closing of the New Testament as a Lamb capable of devastating wrath vented upon unbelievers and those whose claim to belief bears no fruit in obedience.

Jonathan Edwards, the early American Calvinist, has received a lot of arrogant criticism for a sermon he once preached entitled "Sinners In The Hands Of An Angry God." Such a God, like a wrathful Lamb, is brushed aside by modern "thinkers" as impossible. But Edwards had the Bible behind him. There are passages like this:

"Then the kings of the earth and the great men and the generals and the rich and strong, and every one, slave and free, hid in the caves and among the rocks of the mountains, calling to the mountains and rocks, 'Fall on us and hide us from the face of him who is seated on the throne, and from the wrath of the Lamb; for the great day of their wrath has come, and who can stand before it?'" (Rev. 6:15-17). We recall that Adam and Eve sought to cover their nakedness with fig leaves, and with no greater success. The Bible is all of one piece, the Fall reported in Genesis, with all its consequences, comes to ultimate judgment as reported in Revelation. And there is *"weeping and gnashing of teeth"* (Mat. 13:50) as Jesus predicted.

The pattern was set long ago: *"Let my people go!"*

Why?

"That they may serve me" (Ex. 9:1).

Pharaoh did, finally, let Israel go. But only a handful of those who were liberated survived to enter the Land of Promise. And we have seen why: seizing upon liberation, not to self-denying obedience, but to self-serving rebellion, they caricatured liberty into license and exchanged life for death. Having been frightened by the report of the spies sent into Canaan to scout out the land, and blinded to God's providence by their own sin, the adults (that is those over twenty) perished in the wilderness before the march into the Promised Land began (the story is recounted in the book of Numbers, chapters 13-14).

Only obedience receives blessing. The lesson is for us.

For the Church as Israel, so for each one who comes to the Bible and to the Creed, the liberating Lord says: *"Whoever believes in the Son has eternal life, but whoever does not obey the Son shall not see life; but the wrath of God rests upon him"* (John 3:36).

Notice carefully how Jesus equates "believes" with "obey." To faith, this is the Gospel. For, as St. James puts it, *"Faith without works is dead"* (Jas. 2:17).

We are warned not to make Israel's mistake in using liberation as license: *"Who were they that heard and yet were rebellious? Was it not all those who left Egypt under the leadership of Moses?"* (Heb. 3:16-17). And the writer goes on: *"Therefore, while the promise of entering his rest remains, let us fear lest any of you be judged to have failed to reach it. For good news came to us just as to them; but the message which they heard did not benefit them, because it did not meet with faith in the hearers"* (Heb. 4:1-2). And further: *"...those who formerly received the good news failed to enter because of disobedience"* (Heb. 4:6).

How urgently Paul warns us against Israel's mistake:

"I want you to know, brethren, that our fathers were all under the cloud, and all passed through the sea, and all were baptized into Moses in the cloud and in the sea, and all ate the same supernatural food and all drank the same supernatural drink. For they drank from the supernatural Rock that followed them, and the Rock was Christ. Nevertheless with most of them God was not pleased; for they were overthrown in the wilderness. Now these things are warnings for us, not to desire evil as they did" (I Cor. 10:1-5). Judgment came for them; it comes for us; it awaits us, finally, all together.

So Peter sums it up in the house of Cornelius: *"And he commanded us to preach to the people, and to testify that he is the one ordained by God to be judge of the living and the dead"* (Acts 10:42).

St. Paul speaks of *"That day when, according to my gospel, God judges the secrets of men by Christ Jesus"* (Rom. 2:16). Let us, by faith, take careful note that for Paul the "gospel" involves judgment. This will curb our tendency to call the gospel only "good news". So it is, to the "I believe," but so is it not to unbelief.

We must take account of a most important facet of the divine judgment. That Last Judgment has roots in the present. The Word which seeks entrance through our "I believe" is both key to life and omen of death. So the Lord says: *"If any one hears my sayings and does not keep them, I do not judge him; for I did not come to judge the world but to save the world. Whoever rejects me and does not receive my sayings has a judge; the word that I have spoken will be his judge on the last day"* (John 12:47-48).

A legal system serves best when what it requires and how it will judge are both plainly revealed. Jesus makes clear that so it is with Christianity. The measure of final judgment is no stranger to us; it is the Bible we hold in the hand.

"Today" Jesus calls to obedience; if His Word be unheeded, then on the "Last Day" that same Word will condemn the unbelieving.

We have already noted that St. John writes of the risen Lord who appears to him on the Isle of Patmos in this way: *"From his mouth issued a sharp two-edged sword"* (Rev. 1:16). Obviously the sword symbolizes the Word of the Lord, revealed by the Bible.

The Word thus represented as a double-edged sword saves through belief or condemns unbelief, *"discerning the thoughts and intentions of the heart"* (Heb. 4:12). Like the Son, who is both Savior and Judge, so the Word is powerful to save, when received in belief, and powerful to visit with eternal punishment when rejected or ignored in unbelief.

The Word is ever with us. The Bible is ever to hand. It sits in silent, but inevitable, judgment upon our every act in thought, word and deed. For everyone, each act of decision made while it is yet "today" accumulates in the judgment of the Last Day.

We are admonished to take the Bible seriously, to avoid speculations that becloud it. This is the Word by which we are being judged in every act, and according to which we will receive acceptance or rejection in the End.

St. Paul therefore describes his own preaching in these terms: *"But thanks be to God, who in Christ always leads us in triumph, and through us spreads the fragrance of the knowledge of him everywhere. For we are the aroma of Christ to God among those who are being saved and among those who are perishing, to one a fragrance from death to death, to the other a fragrance from life to life"* (II Cor. 2:14-16). The sword of the Word (Eph. 6:17) is double-edged. Note how Paul speaks of *"those who are being saved"* in living obedience; and of *"those who are perishing"* in living disobedience.

It is popular to picture the Last Judgment in terms of some kind of court scene. In this scenario, the Devil may be pictured as accusing God's elect of mortal sin, with Jesus then rushing in to cover them with His cleansing blood. The Bible nowhere authorizes such a fancy. Life is not an Agatha Christie crime story.

We are nowhere told that the Son will intervene between angry Father and suppliant sinner on that Last Day, the "come-on" delusion of some popular evangelism.

Jesus, on the contrary, reveals Himself to be the Judge, and He tells us that judgment will be passed upon us by His Word. All along, the Word of the Lord is exercising judgment in the world, in our lives, in the now that is "today." On that Last Day the Lord will simply validate, with consequences, the judgment that Word is now passing upon us. Or, we may say, the judgment we are always bringing upon ourselves in terms of the "god" we serve.

In the Lord's parable of the Last Judgment (Mat. 25:31-46), it is revealed that the *"Son of man..will sit on his glorious throne. Before him will be gathered all the nations."* But there follows a most unusual kind of judgment. Notice: *"He will separate them one from another as a shepherd separates the sheep from the goats."* Observe that the Judge does not at that moment make those *"of all nations"* who stand before Him into sheep or goats. Not at all. He simply confirms how we all have come to the Judgment. Some come as sheep, others come as goats. That's been settled in life. All the Judge does is to sort out one kind from the other. His judgment simply certifies in what way all have lived: 1) as "sheep," believing and thus obedient, or 2) as "goats," unbelieving and rebellious.

Following the teaching of Dante's Divine Comedy, C.S. Lewis opines that in a very real sense we choose, indeed long for, in our daily behavior the company we will find ourselves in on the Last Day. We get what we really want, either God our nearest companion or God estranged through our unwillingness to serve Him.

And so St. Paul can say, *"Do not pronounce judgment before the time, before the Lord comes, who will bring to light the things now hidden in darkness and will disclose the purposes of the heart"* (I Cor. 4:5). Do you "purpose" to be among the "sheep" or to be among the "goats"? The Lord as Judge will expose that.

Better work at being among the "sheep" now, don't you think?

The aged Simeon, who rejoiced over the presentation of the baby Jesus in the temple, said to Mary his mother, *"Behold, this child is set for the fall and the rising of many in Israel, and for a sign that is spoken against (and a sword will pierce through your own soul also), that thoughts out of many hearts may be revealed"* (Luke 2:34-35). He is saying what Paul said later.

To those who scoffed at His cure of the man born blind, as we have already observed, Jesus says: *"For judgment came I into this world, that those who do not see may see, and that those who see may become blind."* And when some of the Pharisees responded, *"Are we also blind?"* The Lord answers: *"If you were blind, you would have no guilt; but now that you say, 'We see,' your guilt remains"* (John 9:39-41). Those who arrogantly claim to sit in judgment upon the Word, reap the fruits of their unbelief.

To hear and heed the voice of the Savior "today" is to fund for the "Last Day" the glorious judgment, *"Well done, good and faithful servant; you have been faithful over a little, I will set you over much; enter into the joy of your master"* (Mat. 25:21, 23). To listen to, but not heed the voice of the Savior "today" is to fund entrance upon *"the second death"* (Rev. 20:14; 21:8).

As emphasized by St. James: *"But be doers of the word, and not hearers only, deceiving yourselves"* (Jas. 1:22)--a self-deception destined for exposure at the Last Judgment.

Don't you think that the section of the Creed dealing with the Second Person of the Holy Trinity should from time to time be read from end to beginning? Recognizing Jesus as Judge would prepare us to take very earnestly what we confess of Him as the Christ and as Savior. This might have life-altering consequences. Think on it now.

Our Lord's role as Christ, as Lord and as Judge sets a context in which to confess Him as "Jesus," that is Savior. His offices as Christ and Lord and Judge are obscured in delusion by exclusive emphasis upon His role as Savior. He warned of it early in His ministry:

"On that day many will say to me, 'Lord, Lord, did we not prophesy in your name, and cast out demons in your name, and do many mighty works in your name?' And then will I declare to them, 'I never knew you; depart from me, you evildoers'" (Mat. 7:22-23).

And He makes clear the basis for that condemnation: *"Not every one who says to me, 'Lord, Lord,' shall enter the kingdom of heaven, but he who does the will of my Father who is in heaven"* (Mat. 7:21).

Jesus in fact appeared as Judge in the days of His ministry, indeed in every Word He spoke, especially (as we have noted) in his frightening denunciations of the leadership of the Church in Israel, recorded in Matthew's twenty-third chapter. Let us recall, for emphasis: *"But woe to you, scribes and Pharisees, hypocrites!..."* followed by indictment, and done five times over (Mat. 23:13,23,25,27,29)! Forewarned that here was a Judge of uncompromising integrity, the leaders sought to avoid judgment by putting Jesus out of the way. So do all who do not reckon with the demands of His Word.

All this comes to bear upon us whose "I believe" opens to the Word.

This is a suitable place for us to reflect upon what we are in fact doing.

And what is that?

We are going, step by step, through an enunciation of the Apostles Creed. We take, one by one, its words upon our lips. We confess to "believe" them. That is to say, we affirm a willingness, and indeed a desire, to have these words enter ourselves to mold us, to guide us, to govern how we think, speak and behave. That is what "I believe" means.

If we do speak them in faith, they will work their way into our lives, more and more as we think on what they mean and imply. If we speak them only by rote, perhaps saying them with others just because everybody does, these words become our judges, detecting our insincerity.

Think on it.

All that we have been saying about our Lord as Judge can be summarized out of Paul's letter to the Romans: **1)** we are indeed *"justified by faith"* (Rom. 5:1), not by works; but **2)** if justified by faith, then we are called to *"walk not after the flesh, but after the Spirit"* (Rom. 8:4), because liberated to do just that in Him; and **3)** therefore in His power we strive to *"present our bodies a living sacrifice, holy, acceptable to God, which is our reasonable service"* (Rom. 12:1), **4)** knowing that *"to those who by patience in well-doing seek for glory and honor and immortality, he [God] will give eternal life"* (Rom. 2:7); while **5)** to *"those who are factious and do not obey the truth, but obey wickedness, there will be wrath and fury"* (Rom. 2:8).

Yes, the Bible clearly teaches that life eternal is God's gift. But the Bible no less clearly reveals that life is given only to those who qualify "by patience in well-doing," and that this is made possible through faith in Jesus Christ by the power of the Word exercised by the Spirit.

The Creed intends that we know Him in a four-fold way:

1.   As Jesus--Savior.

2.   As Christ--Prophet/Priest/King.

3.   As Lord--both Jesus and Christ.

4.   As Judge--by the Word inspired by His Spirit.

All this we confess when we take upon our lips "I believe in Jesus Christ..." and what follows in the Creed. Yes, it might be instructive, from time to time, to go through the Creed, as concerns our Lord, from the end to the beginning, lest we mislead ourselves.

Article 8.

I BELIEVE IN THE

HOLY SPIRIT

Christianity is the religion of Word-incarnation. The Instrument of incarnation is God the Holy Spirit, CEA (Chief Executive Agent) of the Trinity.

"In the beginning" God incarnates His Word in the creation, no doubt through the Spirit. Genesis reports that *"In the beginning God created the heavens and the earth. The earth was without form and void, and darkness was upon the face of the deep; and the Spirit of God was moving over the face of the waters"* (Gen. 1:1-2). We may well understand the Father's repeated Word "let there be," as exercised through the Son and addressed to the Spirit who realizes--makes real, gives existence to--the command.

Through the Spirit God incarnates His Word, the Son, in Jesus of Nazareth through the Virgin Mary. Through the Spirit God incarnates His oral Word in the Holy Scriptures. For there have been *"holy prophets ever since the world began,"* (Luke 1:70), and prophecy *"came not at any time by the will of man, but holy men of God spoke, as they were moved by the Holy Spirit"* (II Pet. 1:21). *"All Scripture,"* says Paul, *"was given by the inspiration of God"* (II Tim. 3:16).

And, through the Spirit, God incarnates the Word in the behavior of the believer, as the believer is thus led to incarnate the Word in acts of obedience.

All is from God.

All is incarnation of Word.

All is through the activity of the Holy Spirit.

The Church has long spoken of the triune God in terms of the "economic" Trinity. The implication is the division of labor which the Bible assigns to the three divine Persons. All initiative arises with God as the Father; reunion of the creation with God after the Fall is effected through the Self-sacrifice of God the Son; application of the benefits resident in the work of the Son is made through God the Holy Spirit.

The Spirit is divine source of all culture and civilization, of all progress and creativity, of that order and natural faith which make society possible. The arts, the sciences, the human community, the orders of family, government, economic life all follow from the work of God the Holy Spirit, just as all disruption of the orderly working of these flows from the malignant influence of the Devil.

And the faith which underlies the Christian life and comes to oral expression in the Creed is the gift of the Spirit via the Word of God. The persuasion of self which is incarnate in the words "I believe" is fruit of the Spirit. *"The Lord opened the heart of Lydia,"* we are told, *"to give heed to what was said by Paul"* (Acts 16:14). So, too, the Spirit is active in and through each of us who gladly says "I believe...."

That some heard Paul but did not believe, while others, like Lydia, received faith *"by the preaching of Christ"* (Rom. 10:17) was *"that God's purpose of election might continue, not because of works but because of his call"* (Rom. 9:11). So it has ever been, and is now in the discrimination of the believing from the unbelieving, a discrimination wrought by the Holy Spirit: *"But you are not in the flesh, you are in the Spirit, if the Spirit of God really dwells in you.... For all who are led by the Spirit of God are the sons of God"* (Rom. 8:9,14).

Paul goes on to teach us, *"When we cry, 'Abba, Father!' it is the Spirit himself bearing witness with our spirit that we are children of God, and if children, then heirs, heirs of God and fellow heirs with Christ, provided that we suffer with him in order that we may also be glorified with him"* (Rom. 8:15-17).

Saying "I believe..." and the Creed that follows is itself testimony to the indwelling presence of the Spirit. Feel a thrill of joy as you phrase the words. You can speak them sincerely only because He is at work in you.

The *"obedience of faith"* (Rom. 1:5) productive of good works is also by the Holy Spirit: *"But the fruit of the Spirit is love, joy, peace, patience, kindness, goodness, faithfulness, gentleness, self-control..."* (Gal. 5:22-23). It is our own observation of these in our own behavior that enables us to believe in the Holy Spirit's indwelling presence, and we are warmed with gladness.

How important it is, we can see, that we know how the Holy Spirit is given.

While, on the one hand, God gives His Spirit to the elect, whom He has chosen, yet from our side there is a route to gaining His indwelling. Jesus tells us:

"If you then, who are evil, know how to give good gifts to your children, how much more will the heavenly Father give the Holy Spirit to those who ask him!" (Luke 11:13). God the Father will give His Spirit to those who ask Him!! Be one of those, always.

Let us ask in faith, then, aware of the warning of the Apostle James regarding asking wisdom of God: *"But let him ask in faith, with no doubting, for he who doubts is like a wave of the sea that is driven and tossed by the wind. For that person must not suppose that a double-minded man, unstable in all his ways, will receive anything from the Lord"* (Jas. 1:6-8).

We are also warned by a reservation, enunciated by Peter and others of the Apostles when brought before the council of the High Priest in Jerusalem: *"...the Holy Spirit whom God has given to those who obey him"* (Acts 5:32). We are to ask for the gift of the Spirit in order that in His power we may do God's will. So sought as Agent of obedience to the Word, the Spirit comes as gift.

But, if we seek the Spirit as servant of our own desires, He is withheld: *"You ask and do not receive, because you ask wrongly, to spend it on your own passions. Unfaithful creatures...!"* (Jas. 4:3-4).

To teach us how to obey through the Word, and to enlighten our steps in obedience by the Word, the Spirit comes on our plea. To satisfy our own desire to work miracles and gain recognition, the Holy Spirit does not appear.

Jesus Christ, Calvin teaches, is "out there" until the Spirit unites us with our Savior by serving as the catalytic, unifying Agent. So also, the Bible is but information until the Spirit who inspired its writing unfolds its Word like a blossoming plant, like a fruitful vine, like a glorious explosion of Light and Power in our own experience of reading or hearing the text. It is by the Spirit that God's Word lays hold of us to govern our behavior.

God the Holy Spirit is in every way Agent of all natural life and common good. God the Holy Spirit is, still more, in every way Agent of the new life of salvation emerging in acts of obedience in all who believe. Persistently seek His companionship!

This we must stress here: sought and received as Guide to obedience via the Word, the Holy Spirit is in all respects auxiliary to our salvation. He is every-where and every-when at our hand. Not to lean hard upon Him is to rob ourselves of Power.

"Likewise the Spirit helps us in our weakness; for we do not know how to pray as we ought, but the Spirit himself intercedes for us with sighs too deep for words. And he who searches the hearts of men knows what is the mind of the Spirit, because the Spirit intercedes for the saints according to the will of God" (Rom. 8:26-27).

But beware of "charismatic" abuse of the Spirit. God the Holy Spirit is Agent, not Initiator. The Word He uses to guide the believer's behavior is the Lord's. Jesus says to His disciples: *"When the Spirit of truth comes, he will guide you into all the truth; for he will not speak on his own authority, but whatever he hears he will speak, and he will declare to you the things that are to come. He will glorify me, for he will take what is mine and declare it to you"* (John 16:13-14).

It is the mistake of the charismatic movement, in the many forms it has taken across the history of the Church (see Ronald Knox's study entitled <u>Enthusiasm</u>), to suppose that the believer receives the gift of the Spirit to forge new revelations, report special visions, speak in exotic tongues. To the contrary, Jesus says, the Spirit will bind Himself to applying the Word incarnate in the Bible which the Spirit Himself inspired. Spirit and Scripture are ever received together.

What is not validated by the Bible is not of the Spirit! Bear that principle always in mind as reports throng the news of "spirit-filled" this and that, of novelties forever masquerading as work of the Spirit. Test all by the Word. Remember that this is the Lord's own prescription: *"For he will not speak on his own authority...."*

Charismatic movements would put the Spirit in the service of the whims of those who promote them. Such abuse is not for you! Nor are all other forms of "Spirit-filled" delusion. Whatever is claimed as "of the Spirit" but cannot be validated by the Bible is misleading and false. Beware of it.

Let us remind ourselves again that the rage of the Devil against all harmony, all order, all unity in self and society is also restrained by God through the counter creativity of the Holy Spirit.

Is there virtue, harmony, order, uniformity in the cosmos, in society within and among human selves? There the Spirit is at work.

Or, is there disharmony, disorder and chaos in the cosmos, in society, within and among human selves? There the Devil is in combat with God for control of His world.

Just as believing admits God as Spirit into human history, so unbelief makes way for the Adversary of God, whom Adam and Eve in the first disobedience gave foothold in human history.

And is there stubborn resistance, in thought, in word, and in deed, to the work of the Adversary in corrupting personal and social relations? There the Spirit-led believer has raised the Standard of the Word in quiet, determined resistance to the spirits of the age, obedient to the mandate of the Apostle: *"Finally, be strong in the Lord and in the strength of his might, that you may be able to stand against the wiles of the devil"* (Eph. 6:10-11).

It is sometimes argued that the Church neglects, or has until this time, the work of the Holy Spirit. The charge is debatable. But the believer cannot be too aware of the role of God the Holy Spirit in the gift of faith and its application to behavior.

The doctrine of the "economic Trinity" is an effort to codify what the Bible reveals as the work of the Triune God in the making, governing, and redemption of creation. It is always the same God, condescending to our limited understanding, who chooses to let us behold Him at work on our behalf in the several ways each subsumed under the three Persons of the Holy Unity. It is to our profit that we are instructed by the Creed to express belief in God the Father, God the Son, and God the Holy Spirit, the Three-in-One whose is *"the kingdom and the power and the glory forever"* (Mat. 6:13).

Article 9.

I BELIEVE A HOLY,

CATHOLIC CHURCH,

THE COMMUNION OF SAINTS

The Church is.

We know that by faith.

Isn't it visible enough? Why an object of faith? Why the "I believe a holy..."?

Even to the secular eye, the Church seems visible enough, and chaotic enough besides. There are church buildings of all shapes and sizes, denominations galore, conferences, synods, conventions, ecumenical bodies, worship services, masses, evangelical crusades, to say nothing of radio and televangelistic appeals for money with some hints of possible miraculous healing.

What is not visible about this seething vortex of activities?

Obviously missing amidst this veritable babylon of noise is the first characteristic voiced in the Creed: "I believe a, that is one...church."

One? Which one? How one?

Yes, the Church has to be an object of faith if "a" is to hold up. Only one Church?

And "holy," too?

If by "Church" the Creed means model of righteousness, of virtues, of love and self-denial, it is overlooking a vast ecclesiastical wilderness of ruthless politics, shrewd manipulation, sharp dealing, to say no more.

Well, perhaps the Church does have to be an object of faith after all.

And "catholic," besides? Meaning universal, world-wide, all-inclusive.

We will consider these attributes.

What persuasive evidence is there of "one Church" in the chaos of ecclesiastical claims, counter-claims, anathemas, and schisms to say nothing of the competition for money and trophies in free-lance "evangelism"?

No doubt, come to think on it, that the Church must be an object of faith. We learn what it is, not from observation, but from the Word.

And the Bible reveals the Church as one.

Writing of the Church of belief, St. Paul says, *"There is one body and one Spirit, just as you were called to the one hope that belongs to your call, one Lord, one faith, one baptism, one God and Father of us all, who is above all and through all and in all"* (Eph. 1:4-6).

Of this one Church: *"For as in one body we have many members, and all the members do not have the same function, so we, though many, are one body in Christ, and individually members one of another"* (Rom. 12:4).

And therefore: *"...we are to grow up in every way into him who is the head, into Christ, from whom the whole body, joined and knit together by every joint with which it is supplied, when each part is working properly, makes bodily growth and upbuilds itself in love"* (Eph. 4:15-16).

But what, then, of all the visible but hopelessly divided churches?

Is none truly the Church?

It is now evident why the theologians have been led to make a distinction between the Church <u>visible</u> and the Church <u>invisible</u>, the first an object of observation, the second the object of faith.

The invisible Church takes visible form as God wills and the Spirit provides in local congregations. These may or may not be found united in denominational structures and ecclesiastical unity. Which of these come most closely to incarnate the true Church is the question of discernment confronting the believer.

Consisting of children of Adam, the churches visible inevitably are victim to the heritage of the Fall and enmity of the Devil. We have noticed the consequences. Only the eye of faith penetrates the exterior to seek the true Church of the Creed within the visible body. Meanwhile, of course, the secular mind is eager to deride the Church for all its dispersion and division, and all its abortive bureaucratic attempts at visible unification.

The Bible provides what we may call the Church's Charter. It is commonly known as the "Great Commission," and sometimes ab-used to justify crusade evangelism.

The Commission was delivered to the Lord's Apostles, being themselves representatives of the New Testament Church: *"And Jesus came and said to them, 'All authority in heaven and on earth has been given to me. Go therefore and make disciples of all nations, baptizing them in the name of the Father and of the Son and of the Holy Spirit, teaching them to observe all that I have commanded you; and lo, I am with you always.'"* (Mat. 28:18-20).

You will take note that the Charter is all-inclusive. The same Body which is assigned the duty of making disciples is also assigned the duty of baptizing those who become candidates for discipleship. And, still more, is also obligated to training these candidates in the life of good works.

Nor is there a division of labor implied in the Commission, with some touring the country getting "decisions for Christ," or evoking these via the air waves, while others undertake the lifelong schooling of these. It's all one task for one congregational form of the Lord's Body.

There are, said Dietrich Bonhoeffer, visible manifestations of the Church in buildings all over the world where the whole of the Great Commission is carried out. Let those who seek salvation go there. And let those who function in these buildings fully understand the obligations laid upon them by the same Commission. Lacking this vision, the Church has no future.

So, let's ask specifically: why is the Church in the world? We can now answer that question from the Great Commission: to make disciples of the Lord Jesus Christ. No more. No less.

"Go and make disciples" is why the Lord creates and sustains the Church. That's the "why" of the Church. That's the test of integrity among "churches"--is it discipling? Is it training believers in discipleship?

It's a full time assignment. In this vocation the true Church has no competitors. There is no other body created and sustained in history for the purpose of making disciples of the Lord Jesus Christ. No other body is authorized by the Lord to do so. He names its offices; He fills them. He lays out its agenda; His Spirit carries it out according to His Word.

Who is a "disciple"?

The term obviously derives from the idea of "discipline." A disciple is one who is under the discipline of a Master, in this case the Lord Jesus Christ, seeking to know and to do His will. "Making" disciples, then, is enlisting and training believers in the "discipline" of Jesus Christ.

The Church is given one vocation. It is discipling, that is "making" disciples, as the Lord requires. This is the "idea" of the true Church, from the lips of the Lord.

Discipling is evidently a long-time, yes a life-time enterprise. It is what is implied by the Latin description of the Church as *mater fidelium*--Mother of Believers.

Like a mother, John Calvin says in subscribing to this description of the true Church, the true Body of Christ undertakes to bring to birth and to educate for life all those re-born through faith and admitted through baptism into the household of God. Whoever would have God as Father, Calvin says, must have the Church as mother. Meaning, of course, the true Church envisioned by the Creed.

By enlisting, educating and maturing disciples for the Lord Jesus Christ, the true Church sorts itself out from among the many claimants to that title.

How is this education of disciples carried on?

Jesus' Commission specifies that: *"Teaching them to do all that I have commanded you."* Notice the inclusive "<u>all</u>."

The Church is given a program. It has, so to say, its work cut out for it--by the Lord Himself. There need be no concern as to what the Church shall do. That is assigned: make disciples. How? By teaching those who believe. Teaching them what? ALL that the Lord has commanded.

And where will such a true Church, so commissioned, find out "all" that the Lord commands? What provides the curriculum?

That is no secret, really. The commands which fell from the lips of the Lord Jesus while He was on earth are recorded in the Gospels. There are, in fact, a good many of them. And, He no doubt has reference also to all of the Holy Scriptures. For His commands are His Father's commands, and Jesus refers questions concerning life eternal to the Old Testament law.

Jesus affirms the Scriptures: *"Think not that I have come to abolish the law and the prophets; I have not come to abolish them but to fulfil them. For truly, I say to you, till heaven and earth pass away, not an iota, not a dot, will pass from the law until all is accomplished"* (Mat. 5:17-18).

The Bible is divinely provided as the textbook for the Church's use in discipling: *"All scripture,"* Paul writes, *"is inspired by God and profitable for teaching, for reproof, for correction, and for training in righteousness, that the man of God may be complete, equipped for every good work"* (II Tim. 3:16-17). Precisely correlative to making disciples. By divine provision, the Bible was inspired to serve the Church in accomplishing the very end the Church is commissioned to pursue: *"That everyone who belongs to God may be complete, equipped for every good work"* (II Tim. 3:17).

Churches soberly engaged in obedience to the Lord's charter govern their behavior by the divine mandate.

Thus the true Church is discriminated from all counterfeits.

Either the would-be disciple is properly "schooled" in "all" that the Head of the Church commands, or the very meaning of human life and the intent of the Church are frustrated. No fly-by-night evangelism will do. No "accepting Christ" as ticket to heaven will replace life-long teaching of "all I commanded you" as guidance along the narrow way that leads to life eternal.

There are no detours around the Church en route to life eternal. That route is defined by the *"teaching them to do all I have commanded you"* assigned by the Lord.

Those seeking to come under the teaching assigned to the Church by the Lord can do so through the sacrament of baptism.

Notice that the way "in" is not through "accepting Jesus." It is the Church which accepts the candidate for discipleship, not the candidate who "accepts" the Church.

The early church was very careful about the admission of candidates for discipleship because the way was arduous and lifelong. Services were thought of as schooling, and were limited to those who had gained admission through baptism and, after instruction, confession of their faith.

How baptism should be administered, whether by immersion or sprinkling or otherwise, has been the subject of intense dispute in the history of the Church, something we may pass by. But what baptism means for the initiate into the Church is clearly revealed: *"We were buried therefore with him by baptism into death, so that as Christ was raised from the dead by the glory of the Father, we too might walk in newness of life"* (Rom. 6:4).

Whether baptized as child or adult, the believer undergoes symbolic death and resurrection in Christ Jesus. That is to say, the candidate for discipleship is liberated in Jesus from the burden and bondage of sin and guilt, for a new life of obedience to "all" that the Lord commands. We have taken note of this correlation before, now become concrete in the reality of the Church.

The form used for baptism is contained in the Great Commission. Because it is commonly pronounced, and so easily spoken, its full implication may be missed. We will listen carefully.

144

It is striking to reflect that the Lord's formula for baptism enlists the entire Trinity in the process of discipling. It is an indication of how seriously the Lord views discipleship.

The Church is instructed to baptize the candidate for discipleship *"in the name of the Father, and in the name of the Son, and in the name of the Holy Spirit."* The name of each Person of the Holy Trinity is very carefully enunciated.

What does this mean?

It means that the believer enjoys Sponsors, often called 'god-parents,' who enlist through the Church in making the believer into a disciple. Here it is an awesome revelation: the true Church draws God in Three Persons into the making of disciples. That is the implication of the baptism formula.

How is this realized?

It is done through the "offices" of the true Church visible.

The Scripture reveals that the Lord provides special functions within the Church called "offices." Paul speaks of those "offices" required when the New Testament Church was being spread out from Jerusalem: *"And his gifts were that some should be apostles, some prophets, some evangelists, some pastors and teachers, for the equipment of the saints, for the work of the ministry, for building up the body of Christ, until we all attain to the unity of faith and of the knowledge of the Son of God, to the measure of the stature of the fullness of Christ; so that we may no longer be children, tossed to and fro and carried about with every wind of doctrine, by the cunning of men, by their craftiness and deceitful wiles"* (Eph. 4:11-14).

You see how seriously the Apostle takes the role of the Church in the obedient life of the believer. And you see why: *"Until we all attain to the unity of faith and of the knowledge of the Son of God, to the measure of the fullness of Christ; so that we may no longer be children, tossed to and fro and carried about with every wind of doctrine...."*

Are you wondering, perhaps a little impatiently, why the repetition? Why quote Paul exactly the same, twice?

Because what the Church is called to do is what Christianity is for, to mature us into adult discipleship. It's not for whoopla, it's not for ecstasies, it's not for grandiose worship events. It's for making adults out of children through enlarged faith and certain knowledge. That's the kind of Church you must seek out and faithfully attend.

The Holy Trinity, invoked in the formula for baptism, participates in schooling the candidate for discipleship through the three "offices" assigned the Church by the Bible:

1.   The ruling elder: from the authority of God the cooperating Father derives the office of the ruling elder--also called bishop or presbyter or trustee according to denomination--applying the Word of the Scriptures to obedience in the life of the Body. To the elders he had appointed in the Church of Ephesus, Paul advises: *"Take heed to yourselves and to all the flock, in which the Holy Spirit has made you guardians..."* (Acts 20:28).

2.   The minister or teaching elder: from the authority of God the Son derives the office of the preaching ministry, called by the Church's ordination to declare to the congregation "all" that God reveals through the Bible. So closely does the Christ associate Himself with the preaching ministry of the true Church visible, that His promise to the minister, as it was to His disciples, is: *"He who hears you hears me, and he who rejects you rejects me, and he who rejects me rejects him who sent me"* (Luke 10:16). The true Church carefully controls access to the preaching office, as was access to the priesthood in Israel: *"And one does not take the honor upon himself, but he is called by God, just as Aaron was. So also Christ did not exalt himself to be made a high priest, but was appointed by him who said to him, 'Thou art my Son, today I have begotten thee'"* (Heb. 5:4-5, quoting Ps. 2:7). God now issues the call through the congregation in Protestantism, through the hierarchy in Catholicism.

3.   The deacon: from the authority of the Holy Spirit, chief Doer for the Trinity, arises the office of deacon, serving the menial, daily tasks of the congregation and acting for the congregation in charitable outreach. The office began in the New Testament Church with the serving of tables for the brotherhood (Acts 6:1-6).

The believer's 'God-parents' thus appear in the three offices which define the true Church.

Look for them in the congregation you choose for yourselves.

The true Church visible attests its authenticity by the active presence of these office-bearers, themselves obediently involved in the discipling of believers through obedience to the Lord's commands.

The baptismal formula, and the offices deriving from it, have given rise to the practice, noted in some Protestant confessions (like the Belgic, article 29), of identifying the true Church by the presence of three marks:

     1.   Where the Word of God governs the word of the ministry, that is where the Bible is purely, that is obediently, preached, pointing to the active presence of the Son. Of such preaching the Second Helvetic Confession says, "The Word of God preached is the Word of God" (Section II).

     2.   Where the sacraments are administered according to the prescription of the Word. The Protestant is thinking of the sacraments of baptism and the Lord's Supper. In these the Word is made visible, and the serving presence of the Holy Spirit can be discerned, coming to expression through the diaconate.

     3.   Where discipline is administered through the Word to encourage obedience in, and to, its proclamation. Here the active participation of God the Father emerges, becoming visible in the eldership.

The Church displays, we have noticed, both a visible and an invisible visage. There is a real sense in which these two aspects of the same entity seem to merge.

The true Church "is" wherever and whenever its marks appear. These identify the Church as institution, and serve to sort out the true from the false Church. We can look for the Church where the offices are faithfully exercised, and thus the "marks" are to be seen.

But, the true Church is only as a living Body. Where it meets, or when, and in what structure are all incidental. The true Church is in session where and when disciples live priestly roles. That is, where/when chosen servants of the Head of the Church perform the tasks of their "office" in the power of the Spirit. Here the Church invisible is incarnate in event, in occurrence, in act. The "where/when" is on the borderline between the Church of faith and the Church of sight. What the secular sees in the Church visible is immaterial. What the believer sees is the Word of God finding incarnation in speech and behavior.

Given to the Church are the "keys" to the kingdom of heaven. Asking His disciples who they take Him to be, Jesus gets this answer from Simon Peter, who says, *"You are the Christ, the Son of the living God."*

To this Jesus makes mysterious reply: *"Blessed are you, Simon Bar-Jona! For flesh and blood has not revealed this to you, but my Father who is in heaven. And I tell you, you are Peter, and on this rock I will build my church, and the gates of hell shall not prevail against it. I will give you the keys of the kingdom of heaven, and whatever you bind on earth shall be bound in heaven, and whatever you loose on earth shall be loosed in heaven"* (Mat. 16:16-19).

Jesus promises to commit the "keys" of the kingdom of heaven to His Church. The temptation to manipulate these awesome Words to the advantage of the Church has been irresistible. Could the Lord be placing in the hands of the visible church "keys" to the eternal and invisible destiny of all mankind? If so, how? By someone's decision? By vote of a council? By declaration of minister, priest, elder, Pope?

To Catholicism, claiming St. Peter as founder of the diocese of Rome and as first Pope, the Lord is understood as giving to the hierarchy control of access to heaven. This Protestantism disputes.

To Protestantism, the "keys" of the Kingdom are the inspired Word as used in the obedient exercise of the offices of the Church, particularly preaching and discipline. The Word preached, believed and obeyed, does open heaven. The Word ignored or disobeyed stands in judgment closing access to heaven. It is this truth which the Protestant Church hears in the promise to Peter.

The true Church does not function out of its own resources. In its charter the Lord promises, *"And lo, I am with you always, even to the end of the world"* (Mat. 28:20). The believer need have no doubt of the endurance, whatever may come, of the true Church; we recall the guarantee: *"The gates of hell shall not prevail against it"* (Mat. 16:18). St. Paul, speaking of the risen and ascended Lord, writes of God the Father, *"And he has put all things under his feet and has made him head over all things for the church, which is his body, the fullness of him who fills all in all"* (Eph. 1:22-23).

Our concern need never be that the true Church will fail us; rather, our concern must ever be that we fail not in obedience to the Church's task of discipling us.

What is always imposed upon the believer is discernment. Where in all the noise and pretension made in the name of the Church is the true Church to be found?

The indicators we have discussed help in identifying the when/where the true Church exists. But the choice, and commitment, remain your responsibility.

Not all that claims to be Church is the Church. Jesus warns of it: *"Then if any one says to you, 'Lo, here is the Christ!' or 'There he is!' do not believe it. For false Christs and false prophets will arise and show great signs and wonders, so as to lead astray, if possible, even the elect. Lo, I have told you beforehand"* (Mat. 24:23-25).

The Creed characterizes the true Church as:

One (a) Church. Not, indeed, so seen by the eye, but so confessed by faith. We do not make it so by ecumenical compact. It is so by divine creation. The Creed envisions a Church as one Body stretching across all time and uniting its members across all geography. Calvin attributes many of the divisions in the visible Church to "ambition." Other divisions reflect the limitations of fallen man's grasp of Truth. Others portray idolization of intellect or will or feeling. The true Church, visible to the eye of faith, is one Body under one Head sharing one faith summarized in the Apostles Creed.

A holy Church. The term "holy" simply means set aside from and set aside for, separate on purpose. The Church is distinct from all other institutions; the church is set aside for discipling believers. In both respects it is holy.

The true Church is holy, that is set apart, as the only living Body of which Jesus Christ is living Head. It alone is authorized to preach the Word as *"Thus saith the Lord!"* It alone is authorized to baptize. It alone enlists the participation of the Trinity in its offices. It alone exercises the "keys" in the discipling of believers. It alone enjoys the title "Mother of believers." A holy Church! With no true competitors.

The last characteristic of the Church enunciated by the Creed is: Catholic, that is, universal. The Church is worldwide; its scope is all-time and every-where. The one Church extends in space around the globe, in time from Adam to the Judgment, indeed to all eternity.   It is the one (that is, holy) Body to which we can be joined in time for a membership lasting forever. In the Church are all the worthies of biblical and ecclesiastical history, all the heroes, the martyrs, the ordinary. As one with the Church, we are one with all others included in it. Biblical history is designed to acquaint the believer with his contemporaries in the Body.

How, now, are we joined to the true Church universal?

And how to the Church visible of our choice?

To the Church universal we are joined by divine decision: *"We know that in everything God works for good with those who love him, who are called according to his purpose. For those whom he foreknew he also predestined to be conformed to the image of his Son, in order that he might be the first-born among many brethren. And those whom he predestined he also called; and those whom he called he also justified; and those whom he justified he also glorified. What then shall we say to this? If God be for us, who is against us?"* (Rom. 8:28-31).

We can indeed "join" a local congregation of the Church visible. But we cannot "join" the true Church universal.

God from eternity elected us to membership. Believers awaken through revelation to find themselves members of a Body far transcendent over all visible affiliations. But we perceive that the true Church visible has certain attributes which attest its authenticity:

1. The true Church recognizes its charter in the Great Commission.

2. It recognizes, therefore, its purpose in the world as making disciples of Jesus Christ.

3. It recognizes the Lord's prescribed method for discipling as *"teaching them to do all I have commanded you,"* as revealed in the Scriptures.

4. The true Church admits to candidacy for discipleship by way of baptism.

5. It exhibits the three offices implied by the baptismal formula symbolizing the active participation of the Holy Trinity in its pedagogy.

6. It displays three "marks" which are correlative to the three offices: the Word purely preached, the sacraments duly administered, the exercise of discipline unto discipleship.

7. It exercises the keys of the Kingdom through obedience to the Word.

These attributes make easier the task of sorting out from among all the religious activity those churches which most truly incarnate the invisible Church.

Who are the "saints"? And in what is their "communion," that is, how do they share what they are?

To take the second query first: the saints share living in the light of the Truth profiled by the Creed. Saints find communion in the Truth of revelation, unity in the Creed, and one-ness in the revealed Word. We will consider further just who the "saints" are. To start with, they "see" themselves, their world, and their duties in the joy of living in God, *"In whom we live and move and have our being"* (Acts 18:28).

The prophet Elijah, hiding in a cave from the murderous rage of King Ahab and Queen Jezebel, feared that he alone was faithful in all Israel: *"And I, even I only, "* he says to God, *"am left; and they seek my life, to take it away. "* And what is God's reply? There are, He says, *"Seven thousand in Israel, all the knees that have not bowed to Baal, and every mouth that has not kissed him"* (I Kings 19:14,18). Elijah grasped with the eye of faith, in the light of the divine Word, the communion he had with these saints. He was renewed in spirit, and went out again to serve God.

No, we cannot secularize the story. Elijah did not know who his fellow subversives were, nor where. He probably never met them, never shook a hand, exchanged a word. So, then, we may confess a strengthening unity with believers known to God, unknown to us save by faith, who have not bowed to the Baals of fad, pressure, temptation.

The existence of saints is not material for the news media. But we, like Elijah, are to be refreshed in the confession that there are "saints" in the world who share in confession of this Creed and are altogether united with us in so doing. There are "saints" who share with us one Lord, one Word, one faith, one confession.

With the computer era hard upon us now, there will be more and more believers who "discover" communion with each other by way of the *Internet,* or whatever other name computer companionship comes to be called. Never meeting, probably, but finding each other one in faith, hope and love across mysterious electronic ties. No doubt God permits discoveries like the computer to facilitate obedience to his Word among us. Let's gladly use them so.

This, of course, is why the Creed places these words upon our lips: "I believe the communion of saints." It's because we cannot touch this sustaining communion, cannot see it with the secular eye, that the Spirit designs to open the eye of faith to its reality and inspiration.

The intent of this confession is that however dreary the day, however scant the evidence of other believers, however triumphant the servants of the Lie, there are in God's providence *"seven thousand who have not bowed the knee to Baal...!"* The number "seven" suggests completion, all the elect of God. They are here. Now. Feel it. Let it sink it. Admit the Word revealed to Elijah for the Spirit's use in refreshing your self. "I believe..," O yes, I do believe! "Hello, out there, whoever and wherever you are! We're walking together, self bound to self in quest of obedient discipleship! Hello! Hello! Hello! Rejoice with me!"

Consider: what does the Apostle say after recounting the "heroes of faith" in the eleventh chapter to the Hebrews? This: *"Therefore, since we are surrounded by so great a cloud of witnesses, let us lay aside every weight, and sin which clings so closely, and let us run with perseverance the race that is set before us, looking to Jesus the author and perfecter of our faith, who for the joy that was set before him endured the cross, despising the shame, and is seated at the right of the throne of God"* (Heb. 12:1-2).

"So great a cloud of witnesses" too. All the saints of all time gathered breathlessly about our progress into discipleship. What a cheering section! How blind not to "see" them! How careless not to be uplifted by them. Why do we think, otherwise, that the eleventh of Hebrews was inspired by the ever vigilant Spirit?

No the communion of saints is not to be explained, nor need it be. It is known by faith. We are not alone.

How is that possible?

That is the secular question. If we could explain, that communion would no longer be of "I believe." By faith we know because God says so. Therefore, "I believe the communion...." We are "surrounded." Now. Always. Urging us on in obedience, in quiet subversion, in moments of threat and fear. This communion brings to each believer the companionship of all saints of all time.

Which leads us to ask: but who is a saint?

We have already answered that in discussion of the Church. Why is the Church "holy"? Because it is set aside <u>from</u> the world <u>for</u> discipleship in the world.

The "saints" are those who are subversive to their times because they are set apart <u>from</u> the world in believing what the world denies, and set apart <u>for</u> the service of God in the world by living the life of obedience which the world derides.

The saints perform this-worldly services in being other-worldly. That the wheels of society mesh as well as they do, that the structure of order serves as well as it does, that the work of the world gets done--all these testify to the involvement of the Holy Spirit through the obedient lives of the saints in history as it is daily written.

To phrase it differently, communion of saints is the unity discovered in the service of God for the sake of the world, a unity found in precisely the faith that underlies this distinction. The saints are alike in their difference. The saints rejoice in the Word which informs their difference, in the Creed that profiles that Word, in the God in whom they live and move and have their being.

The saints are not permitted to pray, "My father...." On their Lord's command they pray, *"Our father..."* (Mat. 6:9). How often we mouth the words without realizing that the "our" signifies the communion which binds all believers using the same form of address.

Saints find communion in the Bible, particularly as saints in the Sermon on the Mount (Mat. 5-7). Just as the Great Commission is charter for the Church, so that Sermon is keynote to the communion of saints, the inspired fiber that binds saints together. It is spoken to the Church, and in taking possession of us unites all believers into one community.

The "saints" are enrolled in heaven, registered among the citizens of the Kingdom. But the evidence of their presence on earth appears all over. Why the countless kindnesses encountered through life? the ungrudging service? the timely and encouraging word? the winsome smile? the gentle touch? going the second mile? doing without complaint the world's work? all so easily taken for granted. Is it with "saints" that one has to do in these? Only God knows, but the sweet flavor of communion does touch the lips in unexpected places. Better to "see" these as fruits of a communion known only to God and inspired by His Spirit, than to miss the witness: *"So, every sound tree bears good fruit..."* (Mat. 7:17), the stuff of communion, the incarnation of love in human relations. Known to the eye of faith; ignored in the hurly-burly of the world, taken for granted and often abused by the secular.

"Finally, beloved, whatever is true, whatever is honorable, whatever is just, whatever is pure, whatever is lovely, whatever is gracious, if there is any excellence, if there is anything worthy of praise, think on these things" (Phil. 4:8-9). Here saints are united.

God has a way of sorting out His saints. We should take note of it.

St. Paul, for example, usually addresses his epistles to *"the saints at..,"* that is, to those set-asides for discipleship in the various churches to which he writes. So his epistles come to us now.

Is Paul suggesting, then, that all those in the Church at Rome, or Corinth, or Ephesus whom he addresses are in fact saints, that is to say are all elect of God to lives of holy obedience?

Hardly so. "There are," says Augustine of the visible Church, "many wolves within, and many sheep without."

How, then, are the saints identified? God uses Paul's address to sort out "saints" from the rest. He illustrates how the Word of God is an agent of judgment here and now. Everyone can listen to Paul's words, but only those who believe hear them as the very voice of God. That is, only those who listen with a will to have the Word take possession of themselves are the "saints" who hear the voice of the Lord in the Word of the Bible.

Jesus has explained that: *"My sheep hear my voice, and I know them, and they follow me"* (John 10:27). The Word identifies those destined as "saints." It always finds them, draws them out, assigns them duties and obligations, illumines, enthuses, comforts, restores. And only those listeners who are truly "saints" hear. To "the saints at Rome," then, is really to those who can, because they are separated ones chosen by God, and therefore determined to be governed by His Word, hear what Paul is now about to write.

What the saint knows for sure is that a desire to hear the voice of God resounding in the Word of the Bible quite literally compels attention to its reading and preaching. It's an experience which rests upon no evidence but itself, and needs no proof for its validity. Our Lord says, *"My sheep hear my voice, and I know them, and they follow me; and I give them eternal life, and they shall never perish, and no one shall snatch them out of my hand. My Father, who has given them to me, is greater than all, and no one is able to snatch them out of the Father's hand. I and the Father are one"* (John 10:27-30).

There's rocklike solidity in that. Stand firm!

"For we are the aroma of Christ to God among those who are being saved," Paul writes, *"and among those who are perishing, to one a fragrance from death to death, to the other a fragrance from life to life"* (II Cor. 2:15-16). God's invitation offered is either heeded with blessing, or ignored with judgment.

Paul goes on: *"For we are not, like so many, peddlers of God's word; but as men of sincerity, as commissioned by God, in the sight of God we speak in Christ"* (2:17). How common, alas, are the "peddlers" of the Gospel. A peddling the believer must recognize and avoid.

The idea of the "saint," the separated of God, is not only source of unity and joy. It is also indication of the divisive character of the inspired Word. John the Baptist warns that the discrimination of "saints" from unbelief has consequences. The coming Lord, John says, *"...has his winnowing fork in his hand, and he will clear his threshing floor and gather his wheat into the granary, but the chaff he will burn with unquenchable fire"* (Mat. 3:12). It is by the Word that this division is made, and announced in the easily ignored address, "to the saints..." and no one else!

The Christian saint, then, is defined by hearing and striving to do the Word of God. The saint is "holy" in the sense of separation from ways of life spent in violation of the Word, and in the sense of a life governed by obedience to that Word.

The idea of a piety out of touch with life is not the idea of the biblical saint. Sainthood involves simply doing our calling in the light and power of revelation, trying to make each decision according to the will of God our Father. It is He who will reward sainthood in the end.

Article 10.

THE FORGIVENESS OF SINS

It is the step next to the apex of the Creed, the life everlasting which we considered in the beginning of our reflections. Our forgiveness is the heart of the divine condescension. It is the penultimate gift: the doing-away of all that separates us from God, leaving open the final way to beatitude, and the true life which alone is to be found in Christian obedience. It is a high reach of faith: "I believe the forgiveness of sins!"

By this "I believe" we are joined to those praising the risen Lord in heavenly places who *"...sang a new song, saying, 'Worthy art thou to take the scroll and open its seals, for thou wast slain and by thy blood didst ransom men for God from every tribe and tongue and people and nation, and hast made them a kingdom and priests to our God, and they shall reign on earth'"* (Rev. 5:9-10).

The astounding truth, the incomprehensible truth is that through the gift of faith we may count ourselves, here and now and always, among those blessed saints, praising our Savior and our God.

Rejoice! And, in the Word through Paul, *"Again I will say, 'Rejoice'"* (Phil. 4:4).

The Fall in the Garden of Eden with, 'Not Thy will, but our will be done' at the forbidden tree was undone in the Garden of Gethsemane by the Son of Man's, *"Nevertheless, not my will, but thine, be done"* (Luke 22:42), and expiated on another "tree" at Calvary. In the doing, and the undoing, of sin is the essence of Christianity and the scope of human history: *"All we like sheep have gone astray; we have turned every one to his own way; and the Lord has laid on him the iniquity of us all"* (Is. 53:6). So that the sheep who believe may hear: *"Blessed are those who wash their robes, that they may have the right to the tree of life and that they may enter the city by the gates"* (Rev. 22:14).

May we ask, the forgiveness of sins, what is that?

In a word, it is revealed that the just God chooses to appease His own justice, when violated by man, through the sacrifice of His own Son: *"For God so loved the world that he gave his only Son, that whoever believes in him should not perish but have eternal life"* (John 3:16)--one of the most quoted texts in the Bible, and the axis about which Christianity and human history revolve. And this was prefigured by the sacrificial system laid by God upon Israel, revealed in the Old Testament by the prophets as promise of ultimate redemption through the shed blood of Jesus Christ. Long before Calvary it was clearly shown that, *"Without the shedding of blood there is no forgiveness of sins"* (Heb. 9:22). That is to say, the penalty laid upon sin in the beginning, *"...the day you eat of it you shall die"* (Gen. 2:17) would be satisfied either **1**) only with the death of all who sinned, or **2**) with the vicarious death of a Substitute transcendent to all, the Son of God.

As the Psalmist says in contemplation of his own relation to God, *"Such knowledge is too wonderful for me; it is high, I cannot attain it"* (Ps. 139:6). So overpowering it is, also, with the contemplation of our forgiveness in God's sacrifice of His only begotten Son on our behalf. We look back, now, at all we have confessed through the Creed so far, and see how absolute is the reality of our humiliation and how absurd it is to obscure that in garments of false pride and arrogance. *"It is he,"* the prophet says of the Creator, *"who sits above the circle of the earth, and its inhabitants are like grasshoppers"* (Is. 40:22). Not much to strut about. Remember it next time you envy the jet set, the elegant, the over-rich, the tyrant--like grasshoppers all, before the God whose forgiveness of sins we celebrate, yes and we too "as grasshoppers."

FORGIVENESS...   Only God Can

What, then, can be said about God's forgiveness of sins?

First, only God can do that.

That is because sin cuts us off from God. From within it we cannot reach out to Him. That is depravity, little as the secular mind likes the idea. Mankind could make the gap, but only God can bridge it.

When Jesus says to the paralytic whose friends had let him down through an opening in the roof of a crowded room, *"My son, your sins are forgiven,"* some of the scribes immediately thought: *"Why does this man speak thus? It is blasphemy! Who can forgive sins but God alone?"* (Mark 2:5-7). They were right about that. Only God can forgive sins.

But what unbelief could not perceive is that on Jesus' lips the declaration was not blasphemous because He was, indeed, God. They were faced, as everyone is, with an option: **1)** either this man was in fact God, and thus bore witness to that fact, or **2)** this man was a charlatan. They chose the latter. They thus forfeited entrance upon the new life of faith.

But this forgiveness is never a matter of the popular phrase, "forgive and forget." We cannot try to understand our confession of the forgiveness of sins in that sense. That may be what we mean by forgiveness: forgive i̲s̲ forget--no revenge, no hard feelings, just let it pass as if it had never happened. Forget it! So we have to do, it is often said, to keep the wheels of society turning.

But how can God, the omniscient One, forget? How could divine justice be satisfied by ignoring its own violation? Then God Himself would be unjust. One of the grave defects of human society is the willingness to ignore just punishment for commission of evil. Which only multiplies evil by itself. That cannot be the meaning of our confession.

In the universe made and sustained by God the sin which alienates man from Creator must be atoned for if communion is to be restored. Sin must be blotted out in appropriate punishment, not forgotten.

Forgiveness involves, therefore, that God made provision for the forgiveness of sins by *"...sending his own Son in the likeness of sinful flesh and for sin..."* (Rom. 8:3). *"Blotting out the handwriting of ordinances that was against us, which was contrary to us, and took it out of the way, nailing it to his cross"* (Col. 2:14).

In the forgiveness of sins is our liberation though faith to pursue a life of grateful obedience--not to earn salvation, but to real-ize it: *"...in order that the just requirements of the law might be fulfilled in us, who walk not according to the flesh, but according to the Spirit. For those who live according to the flesh set their minds on the things of the flesh, but those who live according to the Spirit set their minds on the things of the Spirit"* (Rom. 8:5).

Our "I believe the forgiveness of sins" becomes the route to living according to the Spirit. For herein is our sinfulness: *"To set the mind on the flesh is death, but to set the mind on the Spirit is life and peace. For the mind that is set on the flesh is hostile to God; it does not submit to God's law, indeed it cannot; and those who are in the flesh cannot please God. But you are not in the flesh, if the Spirit of God dwells in you"* (Rom. 8:6-9). Our "I believe" opens the way to His indwelling.

Forgiveness is key to restoration, just as confession and contrition are keys to forgiveness. It is not to gain heaven that we seek the forgiveness of sins. It is, first of all, that we can live in obedience.

Sinfulness haunts humankind. Alienation from the Creator underlies the angst which gnaws at peace of mind. It is phrased by the Prophet Micah: *"With what shall I come before the Lord, and bow myself before God on high? Shall I come before him with burnt offerings, with calves a year old? Will the Lord be pleased with thousands of rams, with ten thousands of rivers of oil? Shall I give my first-born for my transgressions, the fruit of my body for the sin of my soul?"* (Mic. 6:6-7).

That is the instinct which infuses the human sacrifices of pagan peoples: human flesh must pay for sins done by human beings, only the fleshly representatives of the flesh in which sin is committed can be offered in its expiation.

Jesus Christ assumes <u>our</u> flesh in order that He might suffer and die for our sin. The Incarnation achieves its purpose in our receiving through faith the forgiveness of sins.

Therefore, *"We are,"* in the words of St. Paul, *"more than conquerors through him that loved us,"* (Rom. 8: 37), *"who gave himself for our sins to deliver us from the present evil age, according to the will of our God and Father"* (Gal. 1:4).

The "forgiveness of sins" is of immediate importance to us. It signals emancipation from the burden of guilt inherited at birth and augmented daily through our less than perfect obedience. Like the paralytics, the lame, the blind, the deaf and dumb healed by Jesus, so the believer enjoys spiritual healing in the "forgiveness of sins" and is able to pursue the life of obedience through Word and Spirit.

The Prophet Micah answers his own question, posed above, this way: *"He has showed you, O man, what is good; and what does the Lord require of you but to do justice, and to love kindness, and to walk humbly with your God?"* (Micah 6:8).

Our hope of doing that lies in the liberation from guilt and alienation wrought for us by Jesus Christ, made ours through faith. It's the teaching of the Creed.

Forgiveness opens the way, not only to ultimate reunion with God forever, but offers the promise of reunion with Him after every slip into disobedience, thanks to Jesus Christ our High Priest serving us at His Father's right hand: *"to one...who trusts him who justifies the ungodly,"* Paul tells us, *"such faith is reckoned as righteousness"* (Rom. 4:5). In the promise of that Word, received through faith, the believer renews pursuit of the divine will every day anew.

The "forgiven" arise in joy, and do the work of the day in an aura of thanksgiving. It's a subversion that shows!

It's a subversion grown out of hearing, every day, in the temple of the self, the Word of the Lord: *"For whoever would save his life will lose it; and whoever loses his life for my sake, he will save it"* (Luke 9:24). That is, whoever is determined to go his own way, seeking thus to insure his own 'salvation,' walks the way of death; whoever wills to walk in Jesus' Word, pursues life.

The Lord goes on to say: *"For what profit is it if one gain the whole world, and loses or forfeits oneself?"* (Luke 9:25). O, the secular way may seem the shrewd way, the profitable way, the route to fame and power. And, indeed, even to God's obedient ones these may come, but if these things are won by means that are not God's, then the judgment impends: *"The wages of sin is death"* (Rom. 6:23).

It is the disposition of the fool always to take his own way: *"The fool says in his heart, 'There is no God'"* (Ps. 14:1; 53:1). And that is why the Lord and His disciples all begin their preaching with, *"Repent..!"* That is, awake to the reality of God, change your "boss" from self to God, from self-indulgence to self-denial.

It's possibility ever available through faith, thanks to the "forgiveness of sins."

Article 11.

THE RESURRECTION OF THE BODY

Now, that's a mysterious thing!

Secular philosophies across the ages have announced the "immortality of the soul." Plato and others taught the liberation of the soul at death from "the prison house of the body."

The philosophers of Athens probably would not have been offended if Paul had affirmed the immortality of the soul. But Paul's declaration of the Lord's physical resurrection, implying the whole man Jesus, led to scoffing and rejection: *"Now when they heard of the resurrection of the dead, some mocked; but others said, 'We will hear you again about this'"* (Acts 17:32). Pagan wisdom spoke of the body as something to be escaped in immortality.

But Christianity declares the resurrection of the body. The self is never to be freed of its own body. That is Christianity.

God makes the body as intimate tool for the soul. That the body is never to be despised is declared in the promise of its resurrection.

Why this promise?

Might it not be nicer to look forward to inhabiting, say, an angelic body after death? An ethereal body of some kind? Or at least one of larger dimensions, or greater attractiveness than the body we are stuck with? Even if, on peering into the mirror, we are rather pleased with the view?

But we recall that it was in His own human body that the Lord arose from the dead, appeared to His disciples, and was raised out of their sight into heaven where He even now rules at the right hand of the Father. He is the forerunner and guarantee of our own rising from the grave, body to be united with soul forever.

The idea of "body" has a unique role in Christianity.

The Bible commonly distinguishes "body" from "flesh" in describing the human being. And speaks well of "body," usually, and ill of "flesh."

The "flesh" is sometimes portrayed as the very seat of sin: *"For I know that in my flesh dwells no good thing"* (Rom. 7:18). And repeatedly evil is described as *"works of the flesh"* (Gal. 5:19, Col. 2:11, etc.).

The body, we have noticed, is called *"temple"* of the Spirit. St. John tells us that even Jesus Himself made reference to *"the temple of his body"* (John 2:21).

The biblical discrimination of <u>body</u> from <u>flesh</u> can be instructive.

We all share the same "flesh." We are each of us particularized by a unique "body"-- yours is yours, his is his, hers is hers; we can't even share the same toothache. Christianity is a religion of particulars, each of us taken one by one. So we are born, so we live, so we die and so we are judged. And representative of that absolute separation is the body, each self by itself inhabiting its own "temple" of flesh. Each self unique. Resurrection of the body emphasizes this characteristic of Christianity. You are you, and will be you forever. Not even death will change that.

The Creed does not lead us into confession of the resurrection of the "flesh." But it is none-the-less true that human "flesh," too, is unique. God made it so by creating Eve out of Adam's rib (Gen. 2:21-22), thus making them and the whole family of man of one flesh.

168

"For he [God] made from one blood all the nations of the earth," Paul tells the Athenians (Acts 17:26). The human blood stream is neither shared with the animal, nor derived from it: *"For not all flesh is alike, but there is one kind for men, another for the animals, another for birds, and another for fish"* (I Cor. 15:39).

God's revelation of the mode in which He made Eve sheds Light upon the constitution of the human race: *"So the Lord caused a deep sleep to fall upon the man, and while he slept took one of his ribs and closed up its place with flesh; and the rib which the Lord God had taken from the man he made into woman and brought her to the man. Then the man said, 'This at last is bone of my bones and flesh of my flesh; she shall be called Woman, because she was taken out of man.' Therefore a man leaves his father and his mother and cleaves to his wife, and they become one flesh"* (Gen. 2:21-24).

There's a lot to "see" in the Light of that revelation. For now, notice that in this unique creation of Eve, God carefully preserved human flesh as separate from all other. He thus prepared a "flesh" unique to mankind which His Son could assume to be indissolubly joined to man at His incarnation: *"And the Word became flesh and dwelt among us, full of grace and truth"* (John 1:14). No person, no self, can say, nor fear, that he has no share in Christ, waiting on acknowledgment through faith unto salvation. No one can say, or feel, that 'He was not like me.' Jesus was joined to the uniquely human flesh which all share. But, like all of us, in becoming "flesh" the Lord Jesus particularized that flesh in His own body. And He, like us, was raised in that body from the dead.

God has a unique investment in the human body, no doubt reflected in the appreciation of its beauty in both female and male form which the great artists have displayed across the centuries.

So jealous is God of the body that Paul can say, *"If anyone destroys God's temple, God will destroy him. For God's temple is holy, and that temple you are"* (I Cor. 3:16-17). Imagine the awesome burden of guilt resting upon this twentieth century during which some one hundred million or more human bodies have been done to death by war and dictatorships. Bodies are mutilated, destroyed, abused and neglected everywhere in our century. Those responsible will not escape judgment. For the resurrection of the body indicts such abuse of God's handiwork.

The body is to be revered, both by its inhabitant and by everyone else. Each body is destined for resurrection. Want to pause and pinch your arm? It's going to be raised some day in newness of life, along with the rest of you.

God carefully made the human body to be His dwelling-place, and breathed life (Spirit) into it (Gen. 2:7). Man unhallowed the body in sin, making it uninhabitable by the Spirit until He returns through faith in Jesus' self-sacrifice. Christianity might well be construed as the religion built about the Holy Spirit's return to the temple first made for Him, the human body.

Jesus can describe bodily ailments as Satan's attack upon the temple of the human body. After curing a lame woman, "bent over" for eighteen years, Jesus tells those critical of Him for healing her on the Sabbath day, *"And ought not this woman, daughter of Abraham whom Satan bound for eighteen years, be loosed from this bond on the sabbath day?"* (Luke 13:16).

Obviously, the Devil recognizes in the human body a symbol he is determined to denigrate, and alas how successful he is. The denigration of the female body into sex symbol, for example, demeans what God makes to be temple of His Spirit. And just as obviously, the resurrection of the body declares God's ultimate, triumphant rejection of the Devil's designs.

Among the earliest of God's commands is this provision for the sanctity of the body, made to Noah and his sons immediately after the flood: *"For your lifeblood I will surely require a reckoning; of every beast I will require it and of man; of every man's brother I will require the life of man. Whoever sheds the blood of man, by man shall his blood be shed; for God made man in his own image"* (Gen. 9:5-6). It's a subversive view not popular among opponents of capital punishment, but it is the Word of God!

Your confession of the resurrection of the body is, then. the final stress of Christianity's emphasis upon the infinite value of your and everyone else's particular self, the union of soul/body, of self/fleshly abode.

Christianity is not a religion of mass movements.

When Christianity degenerates into these, into shouting, swaying, ecstatic crowds, it is no longer itself. It is counterfeit. Mass phenomena reflect idolatry of the emotions, not the influence of Christianity.

The Word is addressed to the self. Believing is of the self. The indwelling of the Spirit is within the self. Obedience is of the self. Judgment is upon the self. And resurrection of the body is certification of the enduring uniqueness of each self. And all this is symbolized by the uniqueness of each person's own body.

At the price of the Son's awful self-sacrifice, God preserves the body of the believer in life and makes of it a temple for the indwelling of His Spirit. So intimately is the self and its three faculties united with the body that person and body are as one. There are even a few theologians who claim to see in the body some witness to the Image of God in which mankind is made.

A whole regimen of personal ethic and responsibility inheres in the divine estimate of the human body. Paul reasons from the mutual participation of bodily organs in the welfare of the body to the mutual service of each other ordained for members by faith of the Body of Christ, the Church: *"For just as the body is one and has many members, and all the members of the body, though many, are one body, so it is with Christ. For by one Spirit we were all baptized into one body....that the members may have the same care for one another"* (I Cor. 12:12-13,25).

The Bible's constant condemnation of sexual indulgence arises out of concern for the purity of the Spirit's abode, in those bodies becoming through faith the temples of the Spirit. Paul speaks of the wickedness manifest in men's giving themselves up in the *"lusts of their hearts to impurity, to the dishonoring of their bodies among themselves"* (Rom. 1:24). And to believers: *"Shun immorality. Every other sin which a man commits is outside the body; but the immoral man sins against his own body. Do you not know that your body is a temple of the Holy Spirit within you, which you have from God? You are not your own; you were bought with a price. So glorify God in your body"* (I Cor. 6:18-20).

It is instructive to notice how persistently the Word of God is directed against sexual indulgence done in violation of the commandments. And how readily the ab-use of sex manifests rebellion against divine governance of the self.

Rebellion commonly comes to overt expression in sexual laxity. It is striking how so-called "free love" characterizes rebel cadres of all kinds. Such abuse of the body seems naturally to flow from deliberate alienation from God. And is, indeed, among the temptations gnawing over and again at the believer. Some have foolishly imagined Eve's involvement with the serpent in sexual terms, and there have been others who blasphemously suggest that even Jesus yielded to sexual immorality--whose "condemnation, in Paul's words, *"is just"* (Rom. 3:8).

The strength and persistence of bodily sexual drives make a natural avenue for temptation. It is the form in which the body most readily leads into sin. No doubt for this reason the Word so often warns against fornication and adultery. Our Lord's admonition to the woman brought before Him charged with adultery is ever validly in our ears: *"Go, and do not sin again"* (John 8:11).

None-the-less, and despite all this, we firmly confess believing in "the resurrection of the body."

Yes, we do!

"But some will ask," Paul writes, *"'How are the dead raised? With what kind of body do they come?' You foolish man! What you sow does not come to life unless it dies. And what you sow is not the body which is to be, but a bare kernel, perhaps of wheat or of some other grain. But God gives it a body as he has chosen, and to each kind of seed its own body....So it is with the resurrection of the dead. What is sown is perishable; what is raised is imperishable. It is sown in dishonor, it is raised in glory. It is sown in weakness, it is raised in power. It is sown a physical body, it is raised a spiritual body"* (I Cor. 15:35-38;42-44).

When the resurrected Lord appears to His amazed disciples, they at first take Him to be a ghost. But His body bears the marks of His crucifixion: *"See my hands and my feet, that it is I myself; handle me, and see; for a spirit has not flesh and bones as you see that I have."* Then, *"While they still disbelieved for joy, and wondered, he said to them, 'Have you anything to eat?' They gave him a piece of broiled fish, and he took it and ate before them"* (Luke 24:38-43).

Our Lord's body was raised from death's embrace.

His resurrection is forerunner of our own.

"He is risen" became the crowning theme of the Church's preaching. It was the ultimate guarantee of the Truth of the Gospel. Paul writes: *"If Christ has not been raised, your faith is futile and you are still in your sins."* And then he goes on to say: *"But in fact Christ has been raised from the dead, the first fruits of them who have fallen asleep. For as by man came death, by a man has come also the resurrection of the dead. For as in Adam all die, so also in Christ shall all be made alive"* (I Cor. 15:17, 20-22).

Let us hear it, reflect upon it, and rejoice!

We can find no better way to think about and to live ourselves into the wonder of the resurrection than to use Paul's words:

"There are celestial bodies and there are terrestrial bodies; but the glory of the celestial is one, and the glory of the terrestrial is another. There is one glory of the sun, and another glory of the moon, and another glory of the stars; for star differs from star in glory. So it is with the resurrection of the dead. What is sown is perishable, what is raised is imperishable. It is sown in dishonor, it is raised in glory. It is sown in weakness, it is raised in power. It is sown a physical body, it is raised a spiritual body....For this perishable nature must put on the imperishable, and this mortal nature must put on immortality. When the perishable puts on the imperishable, and the mortal puts on immortality, then shall come to pass the saying that is written: 'Death is swallowed up in victory.' O grave, where is thy victory? O death, where is thy sting? The sting of death is sin, and the power of sin is the law. But thanks be to God, who gives us the victory through our Lord Jesus Christ. Therefore, my beloved, be steadfast, immovable, always abounding in the work of the Lord, knowing that in the Lord your labor is not in vain" (I Cor. 15:40-51; 53-58). That is to say, your good works will receive reward.

So may it be for us all!

We have come, thus, full circle. That last, triumphant affirmation of the Creed was our point of departure in these meditations, you recall: "And the life everlasting."

It is the crown, the fruit, the eternal consequence of all that we have confessed. It is the guiding Light of all that we strive for in obedience to the Word of God. Because it is that eternal experience of the very presence of God which fills with meaning the term <u>LIFE</u>.

What that really means waits upon its being enjoyed.

Be patient. It's coming. Indeed, our "I believe" enables us to know that we have already entered upon it:

AND THE LIFE EVERLASTING!